our sunburnt country

Australian history for children

Revised and expanded edition

Author ARTHUR BAILLIE

Illustrated by MOLLY G. JOHNSON A.R.A.S.

MY HOMESCHOOL

Our sunburnt country: Australian history for children
By Arthur J Baillie. © 2013, 2023
3rd Edition
Cover and Text layout © My Homeschool Pty LTD
Images © Molly G Johnson used with permission from the Estate of Molly G. Johnson.
Image p. 138 © Nicole Crouch used with permission.

ISBN: 9780980508758

My Country by Dorothea Mackellar used by arrangement with the Licensor, The Estate of Dorothea Mackellar c/- Curtis Brown (Aust) Pty Ltd.

3rd Edition black and white version of 2013 edition.
2nd Revised and expanded colour edition first published in 2013 by Downunder Literature as Our sunburnt country: an illustrated history of Australia for children.
First published in Australia in 1964 by Southern Cross Media Pty Limited as Our sunburnt country: an illustrated history of Australia for children

All rights reserved. No part of this publication may be reproduced, stored in a retrieval system, or transmitted in any other form or means – electronic, mechanical, photocopying, recording or otherwise, without the prior permission of the copyright owner and the publisher or as provided by Australian law.

All enquiries to: My Homeschool PTY LTD
Whitebridge, NSW, Australia
https://myhomeschool.com

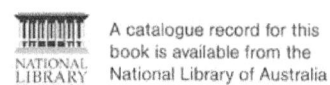

A catalogue record for this book is available from the National Library of Australia

Publisher's Note

I first became aware of *Our Sunburnt Country* about five years ago when I was looking for an Australian history book to read aloud with my two oldest children, then aged 6 and 8. One of my friends recommended it and handed me her copy. She said it was very popular amongst home-schoolers as an excellent narrative-style account of our history.

So the kids and I sat on the couch and learned together our Australian history. The children loved the exciting stories and enjoyed the illustrations. My goal was to read one chapter per sitting but often I was begged for another chapter or two. I didn't mind at all; it was a good read; and I was sounding quite knowledgeable at dinner parties.

When I was asked by others parents what I would recommend for teaching Australian history, I would unequivocally recommend *Our Sunburnt Country*, with the additional apology that it was out of print and they would have to hunt around and find one secondhand.

I was so excited when Arthur Baillie agreed to allow us to republish *Our Sunburnt Country*. I was even more excited when I read through his updated and revised version and I thank him for making this book available again.

Arthur is still passionate about Australian history and has been able to thoughtfully update his original version with added information that was not publicly known and new historic events that have occurred since 1964.

This book will be enjoyed by young and old. It can also be used as the basis for studying Australian history with children. Visit our website for more ideas.

Michelle Morrow
Publisher

Foreword to the first edition

INTEREST in the story of Australia has increased steadily during recent years. Many migrants, in particular, desire to gain sound knowledge concerning this "new" country, and at the same time lots of "home-grown" Australians have come to realize that if they are to say with pride, "This is my own, my native land", they should possess reasonable knowledge of the country's picturesque record.

"Can you give me," an elderly Sydney woman asked recently, "a short account of events that took place at Botany Bay and Port Jackson in the days of discovery? I'm sorry to say I always get Captain Cook and Governor Phillip mixed, and that's because in my school days I was taught much about happenings in Britain long ago, but very little about the history of Australia."

The book here presented should be of great help to such seekers for local knowledge. In the nature of the case, its author could not include much detail in any section, but he gives, simply and clearly, an informative summary of Australia's progress from the Dreamtime of the Aborigines to the remarkable developments of today.

Accordingly, the book merits a most friendly reception, especially from the youth of the land.

History House,
Sydney.
January, 1964.

ALEC H. CHISHOLM, O.B.E.

Preface

When this book was first written I was endeavouring to meet two major needs which I considered to exist. The first was the need to provide primary-aged children with an easily-read, short account of Australia's early history and the second was to help readers to feel that those who from the very beginning shaped our nation were not merely names on pages of history but were living, breathing, feeling human beings, with personalities of their own.

While the book was written primarily for students I have been delighted to learn that many adults have derived pleasure from reading its pages.

In writing the preface for the original publication I expressed my thanks to Betty Boaden, then the librarian at North Sydney Demonstration School, for her assistance in research and her advice regarding the text; to Marilyn Stacy for her careful editing of the completed text; to A. G. L. Shaw, then Senior Lecturer in History at Sydney University, who checked the material to ensure historical accuracy and to countless friends and teaching colleagues who were so generous in their encouragement of my endeavours. These expressions of appreciation are extended once more.

I wish again to acknowledge my gratitude and to include a special word of thanks to the well-known Australian artist, the late Molly Johnson, who illustrated this work so beautifully. Her delightfully delicate interpretation made the completed text not merely a short history of Australia, but a work of art.

Sincere thanks are extended to Michelle Morrow of Downunder Literature for enthusiastically offering to arrange for this little book to be available once again. Amendments and broad-outline additions have been included to bring the detail up to date.

ARTHUR J. BAILLIE
B.A., M.Ed. (Sydney)

My Country

The love of field and coppice,
   Of green and shaded lanes.
Of ordered woods and gardens
   Is running in your veins,
Strong love of grey-blue distance
   Brown streams and soft dim skies
I know but cannot share it,
   My love is otherwise.

I love a sunburnt country,
   A land of sweeping plains,
Of ragged mountain ranges,
   Of droughts and flooding rains.
I love her far horizons,
   I love her jewel-sea,
Her beauty and her terror —
   The wide brown land for me!

The stark white ring-barked forests,
   All tragic to the moon,
The sapphire-misted mountains,
   The hot gold hush of noon,
Green tangle of the brushes
   Where lithe lianas coil,
And orchids deck the tree-tops,
   And ferns the warm dark soil.

Core of my heart, my country!
   Her pitiless blue sky,
When sick at heart, around us,
   We see the cattle die —
But then the grey clouds gather,
   And we can bless again
The drumming of an army,
   The steady, soaking rain.

Core of my heart, my country!
   Land of the Rainbow Gold,
For flood and fire and famine,
   She pays us back threefold —
Over the thirsty paddocks,
   Watch, after many days,
The filmy veil of greenness
   That thickens as we gaze.

An opal-hearted country,
   A wilful, lavish land —
All you who have not loved her,
   You will not understand —
Though earth holds many splendours,
   Wherever I may die,
I know to what brown country
   My homing thoughts will fly.

              Dorothea Mackellar

Contents

		Page
Chapter One	The Land of the Dreamtime	9
Chapter Two	New Visitors to an Old Land	21
Chapter Three	They Came – and Stayed	38
Chapter Four	Rum and Rebellion	46
Chapter Five	Bass and Flinders Map the Coastline	53
Chapter Six	Over the Barrier	64
Chapter Seven	The Riddle of the Rivers	71
Chapter Eight	New Colonies in Australia	90
Chapter Nine	Days of Gold	94
Chapter Ten	Men of Industry	106
Chapter Eleven	Birth of a Nation	111
Chapter Twelve	A Nation at War	115
Chapter Thirteen	After World War 1	120
Chapter Fourteen	The Second World War	126
Chapter Fifteen	Advance Australia	131
	Index	140 - 141

Chapter One

The Land of the Dreamtime

DO you know what our Earth looks like? I'm sure that you can tell it is like a huge ball, spinning around in space. The "top" and "bottom" of this gigantic ball each has a thick covering, or cap, of ice. These ice caps are very important in the story of our world.

Long, long ago – when the world was very young – the two ice caps were much bigger and the Earth was a lot colder than it is today. Snow fell over the two frozen areas and the snow, too, became ice. It did not melt and flow back into the sea from where it had come. So much water stayed on the land in the form of ice that there was much less water in the oceans. As the level of water in the seas and oceans fell, some of the Earth's area that had been covered by water then became dry land. This was the time of a great Ice Age.

Can you see on the map that there are many islands between Australia and the mainland of the Asian continent? In the times of the great ice caps there was much more land exposed and less sea between Australia and Asia. It was quite easy for people to row across the narrow stretches of water. We believe that it was about that time that brown-skinned people began to cross from Asia to Australia. In dug-out canoes they came, bringing their weapons, dogs, and a little food. These people were the first Aborigines to live in Australia and they came many thousands of years ago. They came long before the birth of Christ or Buddha and even long before the pyramids were being built in Egypt.

The Aborigines tell many wonderful stories about these early times which they call the days of the *Dreamtime*. One of the stories told by the Aborigines was about Bohra, the Kangaroo.

There was once a time, so the story says, that Bohra moved about on four legs just like a dog.

Bohra used to like feeding at night and sometimes he would watch the fires of the Aborigines. One evening he saw many fires and heard the sounds of a great corroboree. There were the shouts of excited men, the click-click of sticks as they were tapped together and the thudding of hands on bundles of skins. As Bohra watched, a line of black painted figures came leaping into the light of the fire.

So excited did Bohra become that he could not resist a desire to stand on his two hind legs and try leaping like the men. Down to the fire he jumped and, balancing himself on his tail, Bohra bounded along behind the last man.

Faster and faster moved the dancers until, at last and quite suddenly, the sounds and movement stopped. The dance was over.

After the corroboree the Aborigines saw the kangaroo. Because he had come to their dance without being invited, the men declared he would have to be punished. It was decided the kangaroo would have to move always as he had that evening – jumping on his hind legs and balancing himself on his tail.

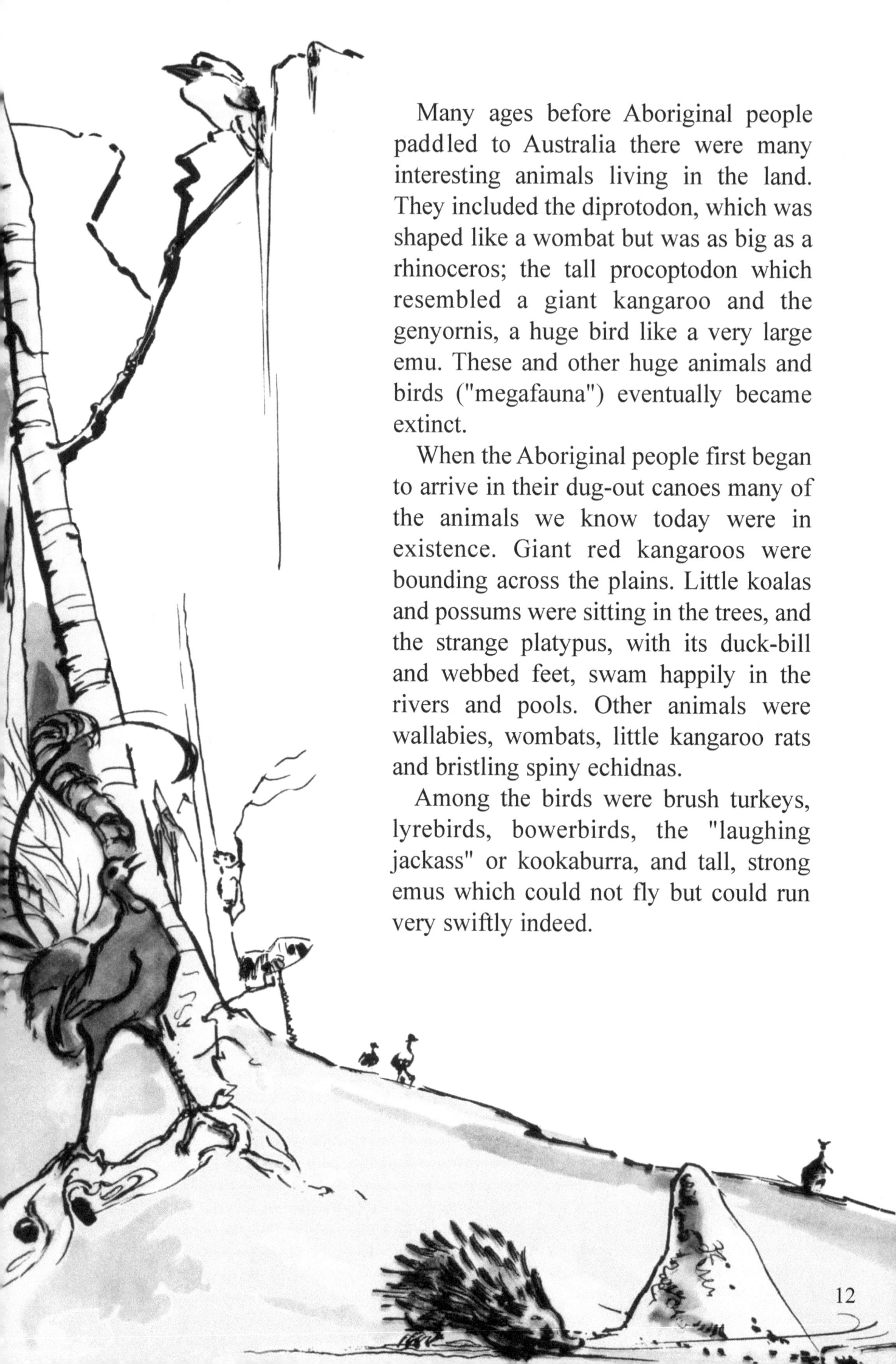

Many ages before Aboriginal people paddled to Australia there were many interesting animals living in the land. They included the diprotodon, which was shaped like a wombat but was as big as a rhinoceros; the tall procoptodon which resembled a giant kangaroo and the genyornis, a huge bird like a very large emu. These and other huge animals and birds ("megafauna") eventually became extinct.

When the Aboriginal people first began to arrive in their dug-out canoes many of the animals we know today were in existence. Giant red kangaroos were bounding across the plains. Little koalas and possums were sitting in the trees, and the strange platypus, with its duck-bill and webbed feet, swam happily in the rivers and pools. Other animals were wallabies, wombats, little kangaroo rats and bristling spiny echidnas.

Among the birds were brush turkeys, lyrebirds, bowerbirds, the "laughing jackass" or kookaburra, and tall, strong emus which could not fly but could run very swiftly indeed.

From attacks by fierce enemies the gentle animals and birds of Australia were safe. Only people were able to paddle canoes across the narrow stretches of water to reach this great land in the south. Animals could not come, and so the fierce tigers and panthers of Europe and Asia were not able to reach the harmless and defenceless life of Australia.

Many of the animals were hunted by the Aborigines. These ancient people were wise, however. They hunted only when food was needed and not merely for sport. By doing this, they tried to ensure that there would always be enough food.

The Aborigines were very clever hunters. From the tracks made by an animal many things could be discovered by these men. They could tell what kind of animal made the tracks, how big it was, whether or not the animal was injured and even when the tracks were made.

If the hunters decided the tracks had been made by an animal that would be good food, they would carefully and quietly follow the tracks.

Once the animal was in sight, the men would begin to stalk it. Light, quick movements were made from tree to tree and from rock to rock. If the animal had looked up, it would have seen no movement, for the men would have at once stood as still as statues.

The animal being hunted would be stalked until the men were close enough to throw their spears or their boomerangs. The whirring boomerang or the hissing spear would thud to its mark, and the dark hunters would then quickly be upon the prey.

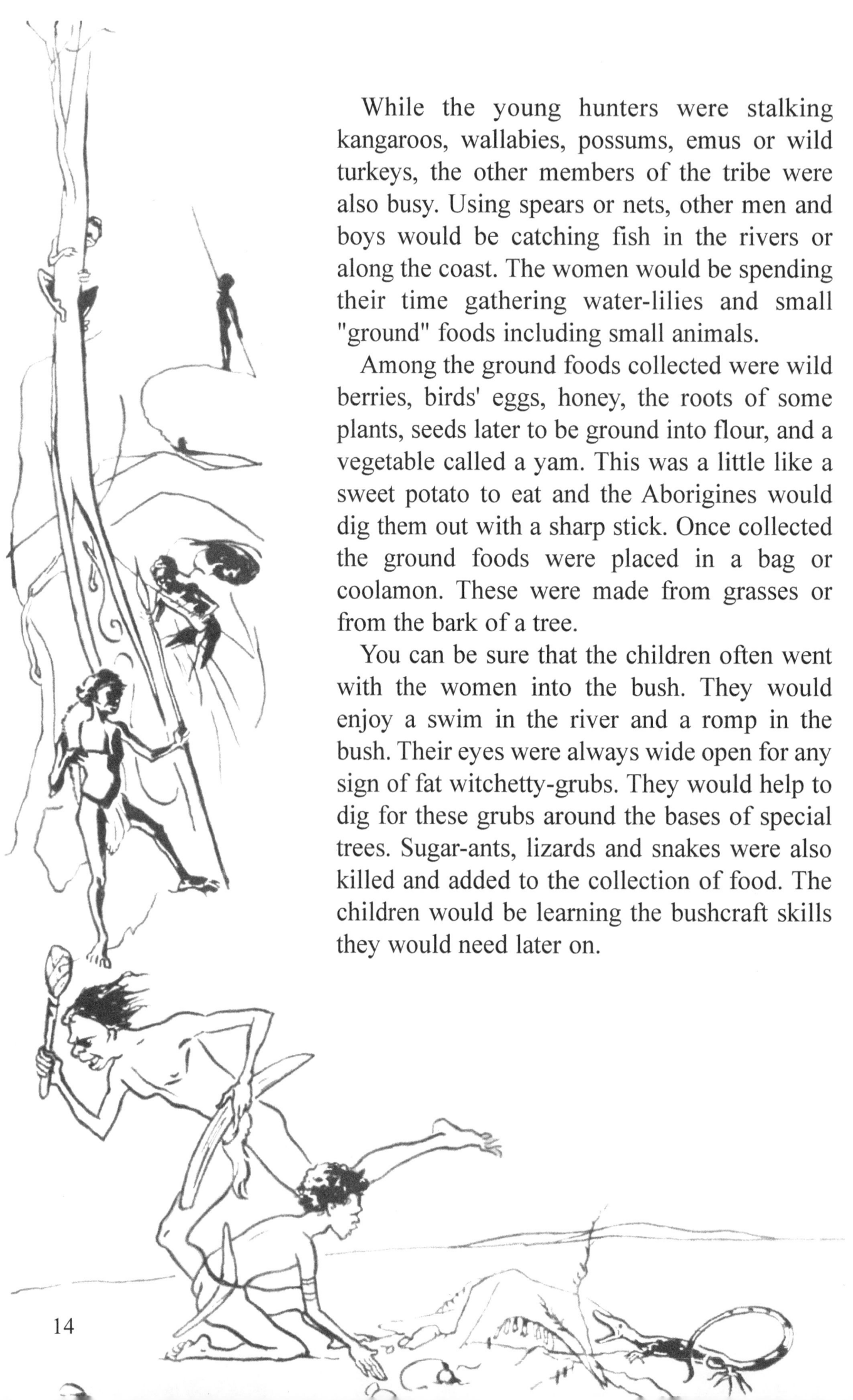

While the young hunters were stalking kangaroos, wallabies, possums, emus or wild turkeys, the other members of the tribe were also busy. Using spears or nets, other men and boys would be catching fish in the rivers or along the coast. The women would be spending their time gathering water-lilies and small "ground" foods including small animals.

Among the ground foods collected were wild berries, birds' eggs, honey, the roots of some plants, seeds later to be ground into flour, and a vegetable called a yam. This was a little like a sweet potato to eat and the Aborigines would dig them out with a sharp stick. Once collected the ground foods were placed in a bag or coolamon. These were made from grasses or from the bark of a tree.

You can be sure that the children often went with the women into the bush. They would enjoy a swim in the river and a romp in the bush. Their eyes were always wide open for any sign of fat witchetty-grubs. They would help to dig for these grubs around the bases of special trees. Sugar-ants, lizards and snakes were also killed and added to the collection of food. The children would be learning the bushcraft skills they would need later on.

Collecting berries and other ground foods was good fun. The women and children probably ate some of the nice, ripe berries, fat witchetty-grubs, or juicy sugar-ants. They would sometimes lie down and go to sleep for a little while in the middle of the day.

After collecting the food the Aborigines made their way back to the camp. There they would share the foods they had found or killed.

Fires were lit to cook the food and to keep the people warm. To make fire the Aborigines used two pieces of dry wood. One was a flat piece with a hollowed-out centre. This piece was placed on the ground and the other piece a hard length of stick, was placed in an upright position on the first stick.

Holding the hard stick between his hands, the Aborigine rubbed faster and faster until little pieces of wood dust were worn off the softer, hollowed wood. Then a tiny spark would appear. Dry grass was placed over the spark and, by gently blowing, the Aborigine would cause the spark to smoulder and then burst into flame.

After the evening meal was over, there was time for the whole tribe to relax. The wise men would then gather in a circle to discuss tribal affairs, the women would chat while they made dilly-bags from native flax and human hair. The children would probably have another game or go for a swim.

Did you know that, long before European sailors visited this land, Aboriginal people were not only in the coastal regions but were living in most parts of the continent? Of course the more barren parts of the country were very sparsely settled but groups of Aboriginal people had learnt how to survive even in areas we would class as desert today. There were many separate tribal groups and the members of each tribe lived and hunted within a special area. No Aborigines tried to take food from the land of another tribe.

Aboriginal people did not all speak the same language. Over two hundred separate languages were spoken! Some Aboriginal people spoke two or more of these languages. Exchange of goods took place between tribes and we now know that tribesmen would sometimes travel great distances to trade for such things as ochre, used in art work and body painting, and also a narcotic called "pituri". At times trading trips of nearly a thousand kilometres took place.

Sometimes one tribe would visit another so that together they could enjoy a dance. This dance was called a corroboree. When one tribe wanted to invite another to a corroboree, a message was sent. Occasionally messages were sent by smoke signals, but usually a messenger with a message-stick would carry the invitation. Message-sticks were usually about 30 centimetres long and had marks on both sides. These marks were either burnt or scratched into the stick. The Aborigines had no trouble in reading the strange signs on the stick.

When a corroboree was being planned, the people would choose a bright, moonlit night. Those among the men who were to be the dancers painted their bodies with red ochre, or with clay. Sometimes they would stick feathers onto themselves, making soft, colourful patterns on their bodies. Strange head-dresses of bright parrots' feathers were carefully arranged. Bunches of gum-leaves were used to make leg and arm bands for the dancers, and special, decorated shields were close at hand.

As the flames from the camp-fire reached higher and higher, the corroboree would begin. The deep, hollow sound of the didgeridoo commenced. Others around the fire clapped their hands against their sides, tapped sticks together or joined in the notes of the chant. The chant was a sort of half-yelping, half-droning song. Soon the dancers were leaping and shouting, and everyone present would be having a wonderful time.

Until the moon hung low in the western sky the dancing and singing continued. Then all became silent. The fires burned down and the people rested as the faint whispering of the wind in the trees and the dry crackle of the dying fires were the only sounds of the night.

There were some special corroborees which only men, and boys about to become men, could attend. Special meetings of this kind were held to show that the boys from that time would now be numbered amongst the warriors of the tribe.

The echoing drone of bullroarers would announce to all the men of nearby tribes that a special ceremony was about to take place. The bullroarer was especially used for such a purpose. It was a long, oval-shaped piece of wood and a strong cord was attached to it. When swung round and round, it made a whirring roar, inviting the men to come.

As part of the ceremony some tribes removed the two front teeth in the upper jaw of each boy. First the flesh was pushed up, away from the two teeth. Then a wooden or bone chisel was placed against the root of each tooth, and a sharp blow to the chisel with a piece of stone loosened the tooth. It could then be pulled out easily. With much singing and dancing and with much knocking-out of teeth the boys of the tribe became men and warriors.

The life lived by the early Australian Aborigines was a simple one. They lived very close to Nature, eating foods Nature had provided for them and usually wearing little or no clothing at all. Their homes, called mia mias, gunyahs or wurleys, were really just simple shelters. They were small and were made of thatched grass over a wooden frame, or of pieces of bark woven together. On clear nights the people slept in the open, with small fires to keep them warm.

The Aborigines who came so long ago soon learned all about the bush, the rivers and the animals of their new land. It was a good land.

There are places today where Aborigines still live a nature-loving life. In most cases, however, they live and work among other Australian people and are employed in a great variety of occupations, including jobs as stockmen and police-trackers. Many are in professions such as teaching, medicine, the Christian Ministry and politics.

It was in 1971 that Senator Neville Bonner, became the first Aboriginal Member of Parliament. Some young Aborigines are students at universities and colleges, while other Aboriginal people continue to produce splendid examples of Aboriginal Art, the best of which have been sold for millions of dollars.

Perhaps the best-known Aboriginal artist was Albert Namatjira, who painted landscapes of the country around Alice Springs and the Hermannsburg Mission in Central Australia. This was the country he knew well, and he painted it just as he saw it, losing nothing of the stark inland colouring. People all over the world are proud to hang paintings produced by Namatjira. Queen Elizabeth II was presented with one of his works when she visited our land in 1954.

Chapter Two
New Visitors to An Old Land

FOR thousands of years the only people to live in the great island in the southern seas were the Aborigines. Probably the first strangers to make contact with them were fishermen from the islands of Indonesia.

For many centuries people who lived in the countries of Europe were afraid to sail very far away from their lands. They believed the Earth was flat and that they might topple over the edge if they sailed too far. At last they found there was no danger of this happening, and brave sailors set out to explore the world. They were looking for treasures, rich cargoes, adventure and new lands.

The first European nation to begin exploring the unknown oceans of the world was Portugal. South went the sailors of Portugal until, at last in 1488, Bartolomeo Diaz reached the Cape of Good Hope. In 1498 Vasco da Gama reached India and finally sailors discovered that they could sail right around the Cape of Good Hope, across the Indian Ocean and to a group of islands where they could take on board rich cargoes of spices.

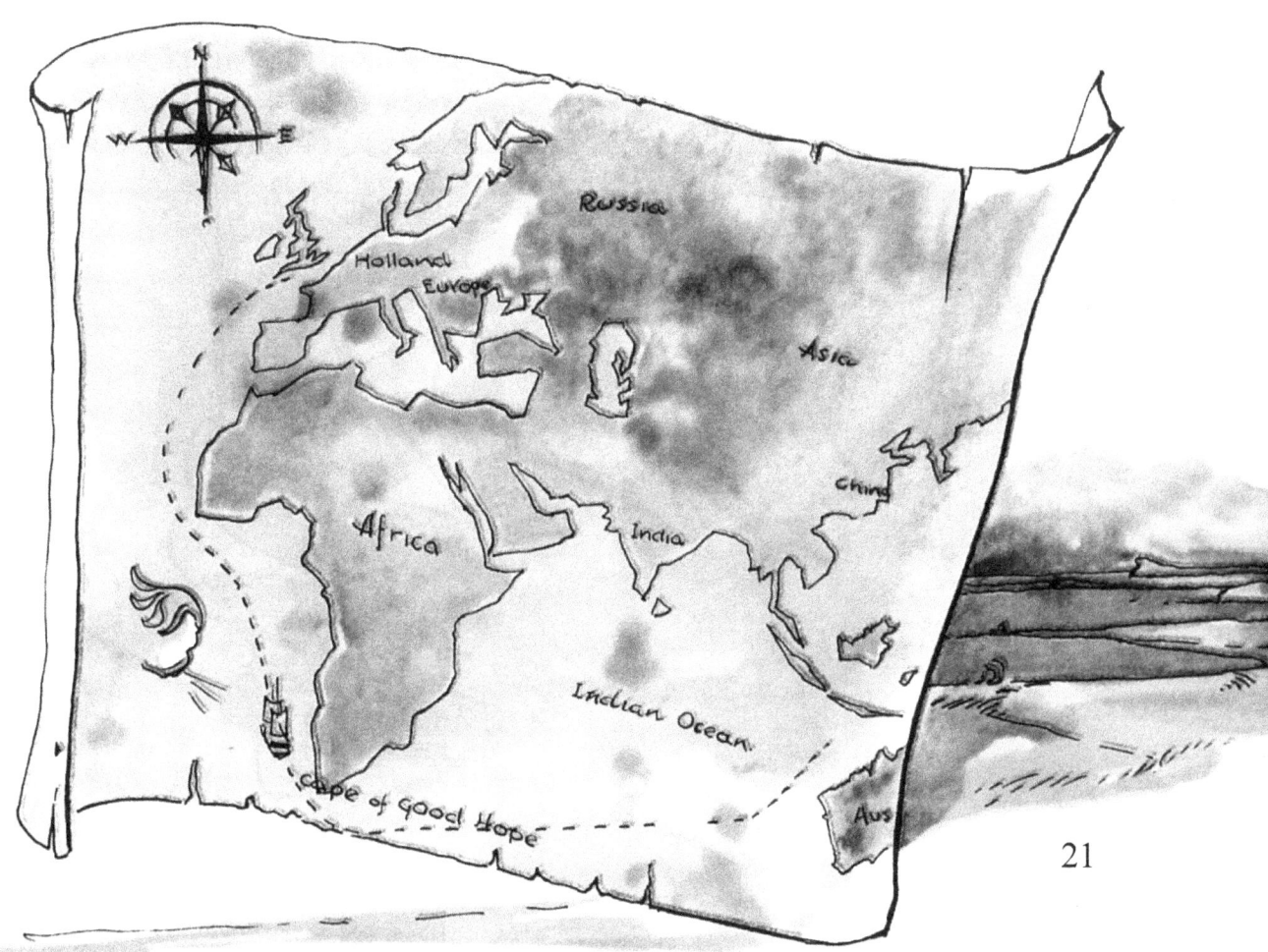

They called these islands the Spice Islands. Today we know most of them as Indonesia.

The Spanish, too, were interested in finding new colonies and claiming rich cargoes. They sailed in the opposite direction to the Portuguese, around the southern tip of South America (Cape Horn).

The merchants of Holland were especially interested in the riches of the Spice Islands. Their ships were soon sailing to the Cape of Good Hope, there setting all sails so that the strong westerlies could help them and then making for the Spice Islands. Their sails were full and bellying in the strength of the westerlies; white foam followed as their ships surged through the waves, and all on board were thinking of the wealth to be theirs when the cargo they were after was in Europe.

In time the Dutch sailors and merchants had built a rich trading empire for themselves in the islands of spices.

I'm sure you can see that the Dutch were likely to learn that there was a large land to the south-east of the Spice Islands. This, indeed, is just what did happen. You can imagine just how surprised the Aborigines were when the sails of the first Dutch ship appeared on the horizon. Did they stand and wonder? Did they hide in fear? We shall never know exactly *how* the natives felt, but we *do* know that the Dutch *came*.

Even though they decided not to stay, the voyages of these Dutch sailors were important in the story of Australia. This is so because they were the first Europeans to make any record of visits to the shores of this land of the South.

It was in a little ship called the *Duyfken* (The Little Dove) that a Dutchman named Willem Jansz sailed from Java to the part of Australia now called the Gulf of Carpentaria. In 1606 he made a landing, but he soon decided to leave. The natives, he said, were "wild, cruel, black savages". One of his sailors was killed by the natives and there did not seem to him to be anything of value to collect.

Ten years after Jansz another Dutchman landed on Australian soil. Sailing in the *Eendracht*, Dirk Hartog was being blown along merrily by the westerlies, steering from the Cape of Good Hope to the Spice Islands. He went too far before turning to the north, and his ship sailed into the entrance of a bay now known as Shark Bay.

Hartog ordered a landing-party to row to a small island ("Dirk Hartog's Island"). He gave them a dish made of pewter, which is a mixture of tin and lead. Articles made of pewter are easily hammered into shape.

Hartog had hammered his dish flat, had scratched upon it the date, the name of the ship, his own name and those of his officers.

On landing, the Dutch sailors nailed the dish to a post so that any future visitors would know Hartog and his men had visited the place in 1616. They did their job well. For more than eighty years winds and rain and storm failed to move the dish from the island. It was in 1697 that it finally was removed. In that year another Dutchman, Willem de Vlamingh, landed on the same island, left another pewter plate and took Hartog's plate back to Amsterdam. People who are interested in ancient mariners and in the discovery of the new world still go to the museum in Amsterdam, so that they can read the words scratched on the pewter plate by Hartog about four hundred years ago.

Many other Dutch ships made landings on the north and west coasts of Australia. One, the *Gulden Seepaard* (Golden Seahorse) sailed right into the area now known as the Great Australian Bight.

Perhaps the most famous of all the early Dutch navigators was Abel Janszoon Tasman. During his time, the Governor of Batavia (in Java) was Anthony van Diemen, an energetic man who wanted to do all he could to make Holland a powerful country with a rich empire of colonies. The Governor believed that somewhere to the south or east of the Spice Islands there was a great southern continent. This continent, he hoped, would be very wealthy, and he therefore decided to send someone to look for it and to explore it. The man he chose for the task was Abel Tasman.

The two ships chosen for Tasman's voyage were the *Heemskerk* (this means Home Church and is the name of a small village in Holland) and the *Zeehaen* (Sea Cock). Food for the voyage, and goods for trade with people in lands Tasman might find, were loaded aboard and then ninety sailors were chosen to man the ships. They were, Tasman felt, the best and "the ablest bodied seafaring men" to be found in Batavia. On 14th August, 1642, the voyage began. "May God Almighty vouchsafe His blessing on this work. Amen", were the first words written by Tasman in the journal kept during the voyage.

Tasman sailed in a south-westerly direction until he was in the path of the westerlies. He was then blown steadily along, until, on 24th November, his lookout sighted the rocky western coast of Tasmania. You can imagine how excited the men aboard the two tiny ships became. Was this a great new country they were discovering? Would there be any rich spices to carry home from here? Were there any great cities to be seen? Would they be able to trade with the people? Would they all soon become rich?

As the ships sailed around the rocky coast, the sailors were probably a little disappointed. No great cities were seen and it appeared that there would not be any rich spices either. The coastline was rather barren and some rugged mountains could be seen in the background. Later two of these mountains were named after Tasman's ships.

In his journal Tasman tells that a meeting was held to decide upon a name for this newly discovered land. He wrote, "This land, being the first land we have met with in the South Sea, and not known to any European nation, we have conferred on it (that is, given to it) the name of ANTHONY VAN DIEMENSLANDT in honour of the Hon. Governor-General, our illustrious master, who sent us to make this discovery." Of course we all know that this name was later changed to Tasmania.

After following along the south coast of Tasmania and halfway along the east coast, Tasman dropped anchor in a bay now known as Blackman Bay. He sent some of his men ashore to explore the land. Included in the landing-party were Pilot-Major Visscher, four musketeers, and six seamen to row the boat. They were all excited about the chance to get ashore and explore this strange land, but they probably were worried just a little about the possibility of meeting hostile natives.

They discovered a fine stream of water before sighting something which gave them rather an unpleasant surprise. The sailors noticed that notches had been cut in some of the large trees. They were sure that they had been cut by the natives to enable them to climb the trees more easily, but the notches were about 150 centimetres apart! "Could anyone but a giant," thought the sailors, "take such huge steps when climbing a tree?" The fact that the natives climbed round and round the trees, cutting notches when they needed a foothold, was not known to the Dutchmen. You see, they looked at each tree from only one direction. They could see only a *few* of the notches this way. Those on the other sides of the trees were hidden from their sight, and for every notch they *did* see there were several they did *not*.

Already a little frightened by the notches in the trees, the Dutchmen were still further startled by the footprints of a strange animal. The sailors thought they were like the footprints of a tiger. Then they nervously noticed dense clouds of smoke rising from various points around them. Tasman believed the land they had discovered was inhabited by people of "extraordinary stature" and it would be wise to leave it as soon as possible. They sailed away to the east and discovered New Zealand before returning to Batavia.

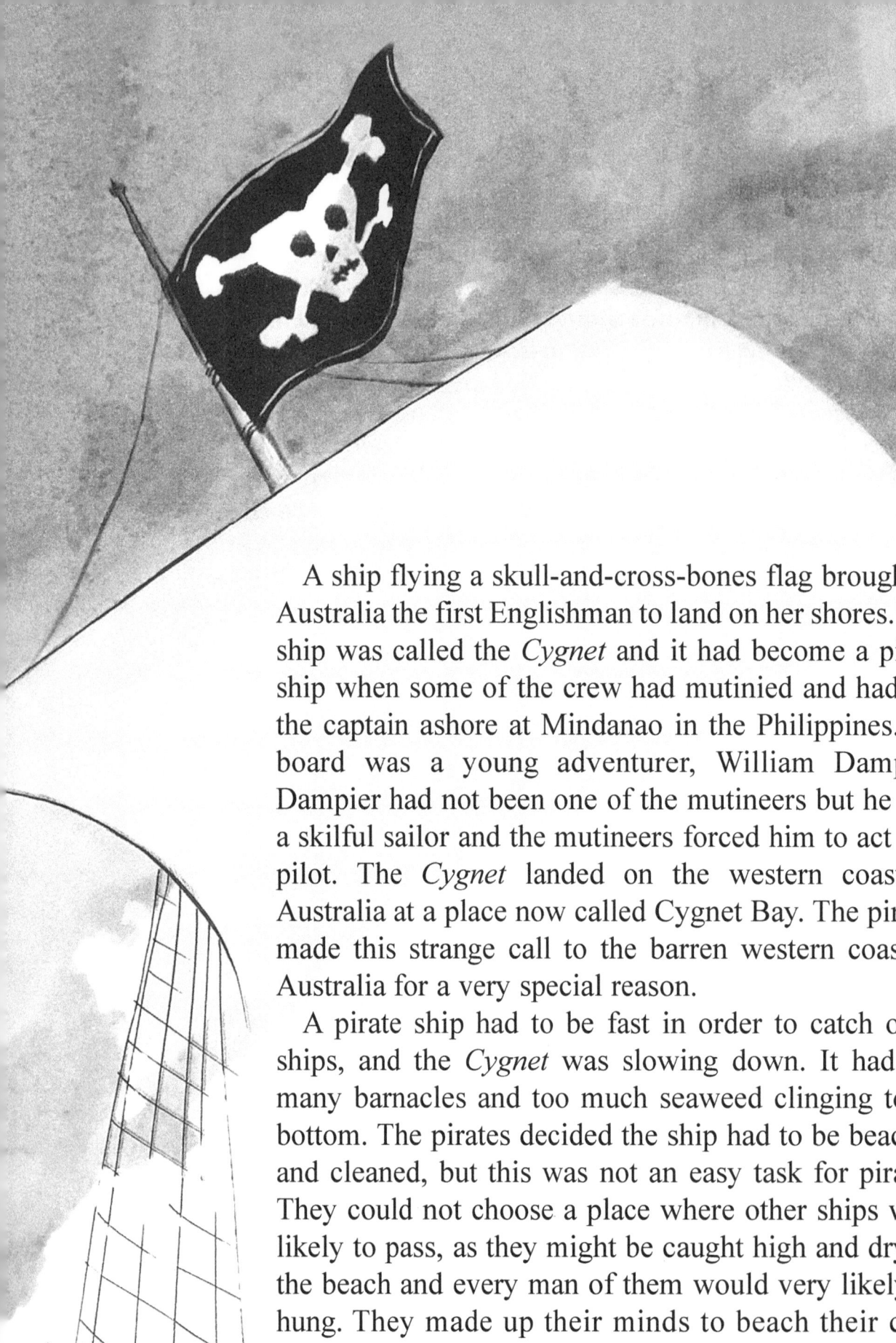

A ship flying a skull-and-cross-bones flag brought to Australia the first Englishman to land on her shores. The ship was called the *Cygnet* and it had become a pirate ship when some of the crew had mutinied and had put the captain ashore at Mindanao in the Philippines. On board was a young adventurer, William Dampier. Dampier had not been one of the mutineers but he was a skilful sailor and the mutineers forced him to act as a pilot. The *Cygnet* landed on the western coast of Australia at a place now called Cygnet Bay. The pirates made this strange call to the barren western coast of Australia for a very special reason.

A pirate ship had to be fast in order to catch other ships, and the *Cygnet* was slowing down. It had too many barnacles and too much seaweed clinging to its bottom. The pirates decided the ship had to be beached and cleaned, but this was not an easy task for pirates. They could not choose a place where other ships were likely to pass, as they might be caught high and dry on the beach and every man of them would very likely be hung. They made up their minds to beach their craft on the lonely western coast of the land known as *New Holland.*

The *Cygnet* stayed in Western Australian waters for nine weeks. Soon after sailing away, the *Cygnet* reached the Nicobar Islands and Dampier slipped away in a native outrigger canoe and landed in Sumatra. From there he returned to England, where he wrote a journal about his adventures. So interesting was his journal that the Admiralty gave him command of another ship, called the *Roebuck*, so that Dampier could pay another visit to the shores of the strange land in the south.

Dampier welcomed the chance to sail again to New Holland, because he knew that the Dutch had already explored the western part of the land and *he* wanted to see what was on the other side.

In planning this second visit, Dampier intended to sail around Cape Horn and across the Pacific to the eastern coast of New Holland. However, he was forced to set out in midwinter and he decided to sail around the Cape of Good Hope, as the route around Cape Horn is a cold, dangerous one in mid-winter. His ship, the *Roebuck*, rounded the Cape of Good Hope and was then blown along by the westerlies to New Holland.

Dampier saw some of the north-west coast already visited by the Dutchmen. He tried to sail around New Guinea and then along the unknown eastern coast. What a pity he did not succeed! But this was not to be. The weather grew worse and Dampier's old ship was leaking badly. Dampier had to turn back without seeing any of the fertile eastern coast.

You might perhaps be wondering why we bother remembering these trips of Dampier's. He certainly did not discover anything new. However, his trips were very important, because it was largely as a result of his voyages that the huge, silent land known as New Holland was allowed to sleep on for almost another hundred years. Why was this the case? Well, you see, on his return to England, Dampier wrote interesting books about his journeys. In them he described the natives of New Holland as poor, miserable creatures, and he said that the land was barren and worthless.

Describing the natives, Dampier said they were "the most miserable people in the world . . . who, setting aside their shape, differ little from the brutes".

Of course, we know today that Dampier did not give a full or completely true picture of either the land or the natives, but people in England at the time did not know this, and, once they had read his words, was it any wonder they were in no hurry to settle in New Holland?

There was a special reason for the visit of the next English navigator to New Holland. It was in the year 1769 that the planet Venus was due to pass between the earth and the sun. This is called the transit of the planet Venus. English scientists very much wanted to study the transit under the best possible conditions.

They thought that the Pacific island known as Tahiti would be the best place for the study, and so they decided to send a ship to that island. The British Government agreed to help them, and a ship and captain to sail her were chosen. The ship was the *Endeavour* a sturdy little coal-carrier, built to withstand the lashings of the wildest ocean and the strength of the fiercest storms. The man chosen was Lieutenant James Cook.

Of all the sailors in the British navy why was it that James Cook was chosen to lead this very important expedition? There were several reasons, an important one being that Cook had proved himself to be an extremely accurate navigator. When Wolfe planned to attack the French in Quebec, in Canada, he needed good maps of the St. Lawrence River. There were none available, and so James Cook was asked to prepare some. This was a most difficult and dangerous task. On the banks of the river and in the forests beyond the banks, hostile eyes were always watching. There would be a swift death for any Englishman caught in boats on the river. Yet for three nights James Cook and a handful of chosen oarsmen silently, dangerously rowed along the river, so that Cook could draw his map of the banks and the depths of the river at intervals of every nine metres. He completed the task just in time. On the third night his boat *was* seen — by an Indian. Cook gave the order to turn the boat around and head back down the river. Already Indian canoes were swarming from the banks. How the British oarsmen rowed that night! Just in time did they beach their boat and disappear into the forest near Wolfe's headquarters. Already Indian arrows were singing through the air. But Cook and his men did escape, and the map Cook had drawn was soon to help Wolfe conquer the French in Quebec.

As well as being an excellent navigator, Cook was a fine leader, a wonderful sailor, and was interested in astronomy (the study of the stars). So, you see, he was a natural choice to be leader of the expedition to Tahiti.

In the little *Endeavour* Cook rounded Cape Horn and set full sail for the lovely Pacific island of Tahiti. He reached the island, observed the transit of Venus, and then set out to complete yet another task.

He had been ordered to look for that great South Land that some men thought to exist in the South Pacific Ocean, perhaps somewhere between Cape Horn and New Zealand. Of course Cook found no great southern continent anywhere between Cape Horn and New Zealand but he did prove that New Zealand was made up of two main islands. He sailed right around both islands in order to prove this. Today the strait between the North Island and South Island of New Zealand is called Cook Strait to honour the great navigator.

Cook had really completed the tasks he had been set, and he would now have been quite free to sail before the westerlies back to Cape Horn and so to England. However, there was another mystery that Cook decided he wanted to solve for himself. No one so far had visited the eastern coast of New Holland, and so James Cook set out to do so.

When land birds were seen again, wheeling and swooping in the air, the men of the *Endeavour* knew that land itself would be seen before many hours had passed. Cook was very excited when he went to bed that evening. In his journal he wrote, "I feel that I stand on the brink of a great revelation." How right he was! His decision to see the eastern coast of New Holland led within a very few years to the first settlement of Europeans in Australia.

It was early in the morning of 20th April, 1770, that Lieutenant Hicks, officer of the morning watch, sighted land. The point of land which he saw was named Point Hicks, by Cook.

For nine days the *Endeavour* sailed north, her officers searching for a harbour. At last a wide, open bay was sighted and Cook decided to make a landing.

A party of thirty men was chosen to row to the shore. As they approached land a group of natives, who had been cooking fish on the beach, made an attempt to attack the strangers. Shots fired over the heads of the natives frightened them away and the men of the *Endeavour* were able to land. While they were on shore, the Englishmen found a stream of fresh water and filled the ship's barrels. Joseph Banks, a botanist (a person who studies plants) had a wonderful time collecting plants he had never seen before. Indeed, no European had ever seen some of the plants discovered by Banks.

Some of the men were given permission to catch as many fish as they could. While doing this, they managed to catch two large stingrays. Of course this was quite an occasion — the men had been eating biscuits and salt meat for weeks. The change to eating a meal of good, fresh stingray was really appreciated. Cook decided to call the bay

in which they were anchored Stingray Bay, but later he renamed it Botany Bay because Banks had found so many interesting plants there.

One of the strange, new plants discovered by Banks was an evergreen shrub with large, yellowish flowers shaped something like a bottle brush. This plant is now called the banksia after its discoverer.

Sadly, one of the seamen, named Forby Sutherland, died of consumption on 30th April and became the first Englishman to be buried in this country. The place where he is buried is called Sutherland Point to this day.

When the *Endeavour* moved out of Botany Bay, Cook decided to continue on his northward journey along the coast. As he sailed, Cook drew some wonderful charts and gave names to many bays and inlets. Then something happened which almost meant disaster for the little *Endeavour*, the loss of all Cook's journals and charts and a story about Australia that would almost certainly have been very different to the one you are reading.

It was almost midnight on June 11th and Cook was resting when, suddenly, there was a dreadful crash. Timbers splintered and the little ship shuddered violently. She had been holed by a sharp, jutting edge of coral. The *Endeavour* was off the coast of what we now know as Queensland.

Cook was soon on deck and was giving orders in a cool, calm manner. He ordered that the ballast (heavy material) be thrown overboard to lighten the ship. Then some of the guns were heaved into the ocean, and, finally, some of the precious stores were sent splashing over the side. At last the tiny ship broke free from the reef.

Fortunately, the piece of coral that had caused all the trouble remained firmly in the side of the ship. This stopped some of the water from pouring in. Wool and oakum (unravelled rope) were mixed together and placed loosely onto a sail stretched flat upon the deck. Over this a mixture "of sheep's dung and other filth" was thrown. When one side of the sail was lowered over the side and passed under the ship some of the mixture was sucked off the sail by the flow of water into the hold of the ship and was then held in place by fastening the sail. To the surprise and relief of all on board these actions proved to be completely successful. Cook wrote in his diary, "In about a quarter of an hour, to our great surprise, the ship was pumped dry, and, upon letting the pumps stand, she was found to make very little water."

Into the mouth of a river sailed the damaged little *Endeavour* and there she was beached for repairs. When the ship was examined, Cook found that the hole made by the coral was large enough "to have sunk a ship with twice our pumps. The coral rock had cut through the plank, and deep into one of the timbers, smoothing the gashes before it so that the whole might easily be imagined to have been cut with an axe."

In spite of the size of the hole, the carpenters assured Cook that no very serious damage had been done by the coral and that repair would not be difficult. Cook therefore gave them orders to go ahead and make whatever repairs they thought necessary. While the carpenters were at work, Banks gathered still more strange plants for his collection.

Cook named the river where the repairs had taken place the Endeavour River, and set out once more in a northerly direction. Carefully he steered his course away from the treacherous coral reefs until, at last, the tip of Cape York Peninsula was reached. As the tiny sailing-ship rose and fell on the swelling seas of Torres Strait, Cook decided to make a landing on a small island just off the mainland coast. On this island, now called Possession Island, Cook ordered the British flag to be raised and claimed for England all the land he had discovered in the south. Three cheers and volleys of musket-fire were sounded to mark the occasion, and then the sailors set their course for Java. From Java they sailed around the Cape of Good Hope and back to England. At last, in July, 1771, the weary little ship and the brave men aboard her came home, after being away for almost three years! How excited the men must have been! How happy were their families to see them alive and well after such a long time and after such an adventure!

Chapter Three
They Came — and Stayed

THERE can be no doubt that Cook's decision to explore the eastern coast of New Holland before returning to England changed the whole history of this country. If a navigator from some other country had seen it first, then Australia could easily have been settled by the Portuguese, the Dutch, or the French. Instead, Cook's voyage in a little ship not quite thirty-three metres long meant that England would have the chance of settling a fine, new country. Quite unlike Dampier and other earlier explorers, Cook and Banks were able to see that the eastern coast of New Holland was quite fertile and *worth* settling. Just eighteen years after Cook's voyage the British Government decided to make a settlement at Botany Bay. There was a special reason for this decision.

In the year 1775 war broke out in the British colonies of America. The colonists wanted to break away from British rule and govern themselves. The British Government wished to stop them doing this and war resulted. For some time England had been sending hundreds of convicts (criminals) every year to America, where they were made to work for a certain number of years. Of course, once war broke out in America, it was no longer possible to send the convicts there. A different place had to be found. After several other places were tried and found to be unsuitable, it was decided to follow the advice of Sir Joseph Banks to send the convicts to Botany Bay.

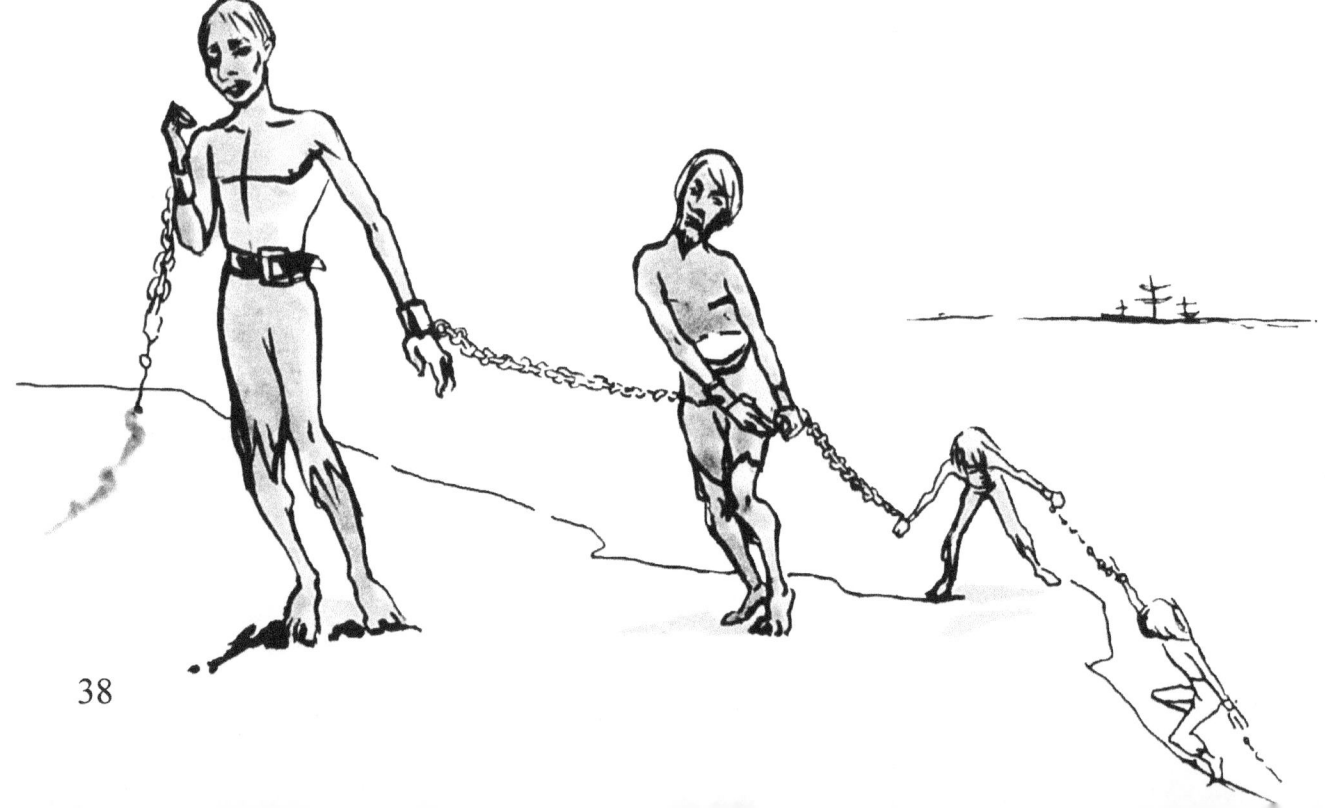

The people who now live in the fine, sunny land of Australia should always be grateful that Captain Arthur Phillip was chosen as the Governor of the first settlement. Others in England considered the new country to be just a dumping ground for the convicts — the criminals of England. Fortunately, Phillip did not agree with this. He could see that the new land could one day grow to be a fine nation of which Great Britain could be proud. He was determined to do what he could to give the nation a good start.

For months preparations for the voyage were made. Phillip could be seen on the ships, in the stores, on the wharves and in the offices of the government officials. He did not spare himself, but tried to make certain that everything was properly done before the voyage began.

It was on 13th May 1787, that eleven little ships slipped away from the shores of England on a voyage that was to take them half-way around the world. Two of the ships were warships, three were store ships, and six were transports. On board were nearly 1,500 people, more than half of them convicts. Among the rest were marines sent to guard the new settlement. After a voyage of seven months the little ships arrived at Botany Bay. As the people on board looked out upon this new land, there must have been many who wondered if they would ever again be able to leave the land which, to them, was to be a prison for years to come. Some of the convicts were quite hardened criminals who fully deserved their punishment but many others were guilty of only petty offences which today would receive the punishment of only a small fine or even just a warning to be of good behaviour in future.

Almost at once Phillip's difficulties began. He could see immediately that Botany Bay was not a suitable place for a settlement. The soil was too sandy for growing crops, while the bay was very open and shallow, even a long distance from the shore. This would mean that ships would not be able to get close to the shore to unload their cargoes, nor would they be safe at anchor when stormy winds blew across the open bay. Phillip decided to search for a better place for his settlement.

Captain Cook had marked *Port Jackson* on his charts. Although he had sighted the opening, Cook had not explored the harbour, so Phillip decided to do so. He was delighted with what he found. Phillip said that the harbour which he found was "the finest in the world, in which a thousand ships of the line may ride in perfect security". The soil, too, was better than the soil at Botany Bay and there was a little stream of fresh water to provide for the needs of the colonists. It was a quiet little stream, bubbling its way softly over rocks and between banks covered by Sydney red-gums, wattles, and bottlebrushes. Called by Phillip the Tank Stream, it was to provide the colony with water until 1826. Today, no one can see the course of this little river, because it now runs under the streets of Sydney, almost parallel with George Street, until finally it empties into Sydney Cove.

Phillip chose the shores of a little inlet of the magnificent harbour as the site for his settlement. He called it Sydney Cove, and the ships of the fleet were ordered to sail from Botany Bay to this new site. As two French ships, *La Boussole* and *L'Astrolabe* under the command of Monsieur La Perouse were seen to be approaching Botany Bay, Phillip had left orders that the English flag was to be flown on Sutherland Point as a sign of British ownership.

Phillip and the men of the *Supply* were already at anchor in Port Jackson and early in the morning on the same day, the 26th January, 1788, the Governor went ashore at Sydney Cove with a group of officers and a troop of marines. The special flag raising ceremony was held there. Phillip declared the land to be the possession of King George III of Great Britain. The guns boomed a salute, toasts were drunk. There were three rousing cheers and a new British colony was born. The rest of the fleet sailed into the harbour later the same day. Australian people now have special celebrations on the 26th of January every year. The day chosen by Phillip to raise the flag on a new land is honoured as *Australia Day*.

Phillip remained Governor of New South Wales until 1792. During that time he had to solve many problems. Try to imagine for a moment just how tremendous was the task he had to face. He was supposed to govern a convict settlement, in which the convicts did not want to work, and in which food was scarce and early crops failed. Tools sent out in the ships of the first fleet were found to be of poor quality, and most of the seed had become so heated during the voyage that it rotted in the ground and harvests were very poor. Sickness amongst the convicts and a dreadful outbreak of small-pox, which resulted in the death of many Aboriginal people, were enormous challenges for Phillip and his doctors.

Some of these trials would have been easier for Phillip to bear if each of his seconds-in-command had been more supportive. But the Lieutenant-Governors (at first Major Ross and later Major Grose) were also Commanders of the Marines and of the New South Wales Corps and they both encouraged their men in a stubborn determination not to supervise the convicts at work, thus adding to Phillip's problems

Against all his problems Phillip struggled manfully, never doubting that the colony would one day be successful. He rationed food, and everyone, including himself, was given the same ration. He looked for, and found, sections of land which were fertile. He encouraged those who wanted to farm the land and had the satisfaction of seeing the harvest gathered by James Ruse at a farm in Parramatta. Ruse had been a convict, but Phillip could see that he was a dependable man and he gave him the chance to farm. Once given the opportunity, Ruse was able to show that crops could be grown here.

In 1837 James Ruse died. He was buried in the Cemetery of St John's at Campbelltown. On his tombstone the following little verse is inscribed:

> *My Mother Reread Me Tenderley*
> *With Me She Took Much Paines,*
> *And When I Arived In This Coelney*
> *I Sowd The Forst Grain And Now*
> *With My Hevenly Father I Hope*
> *For Ever To Remain.*

As you can see, the spelling is strange, but the thoughts are true, for Ruse was a good man and our first successful farmer.

Phillip was indeed a great Governor. He ruled firmly, but justly, and all people felt that he was good, steadfast, courageous and kind. In 1792, when he sailed away from Sydney Cove, he was satisfied that he

had faithfully completed the task he had been given. The colony was now firmly established and most of the serious problems had been overcome.

As he sailed towards the Heads of Port Jackson, many thoughts must have crowded into Phillip's mind. No doubt he wondered if there were any other fine harbours, like Port Jackson, along the coasts of this new, vast continent. He must have wondered just what lay beyond the rugged range of highlands to the west of the settlement. Were there any fine rivers to be found? How much of the land could be used for farming? Did the soil hold great riches of mineral wealth? Above all, would this little colony, which he had worked so hard to establish, continue to grow so that one day this new land would become a great nation? Some of these questions were very soon to be answered.

About the work of Phillip, S. Eliot Napier wrote these thoughtful lines:

> *Phillip, the grave and generous gentleman,*
> *Great-hearted captain of a motley crew,*
> *Into the calm, encircled waters drew*
> *His sea-scarr'd ships. There, where the streamlet ran,*
> *To meet the sands beneath a bracken'd fan,*
> *He set the flag and there a city grew;*
> *And there, from wilted seed, perchance, but true*
> *To its great type, our nationhood begins.*

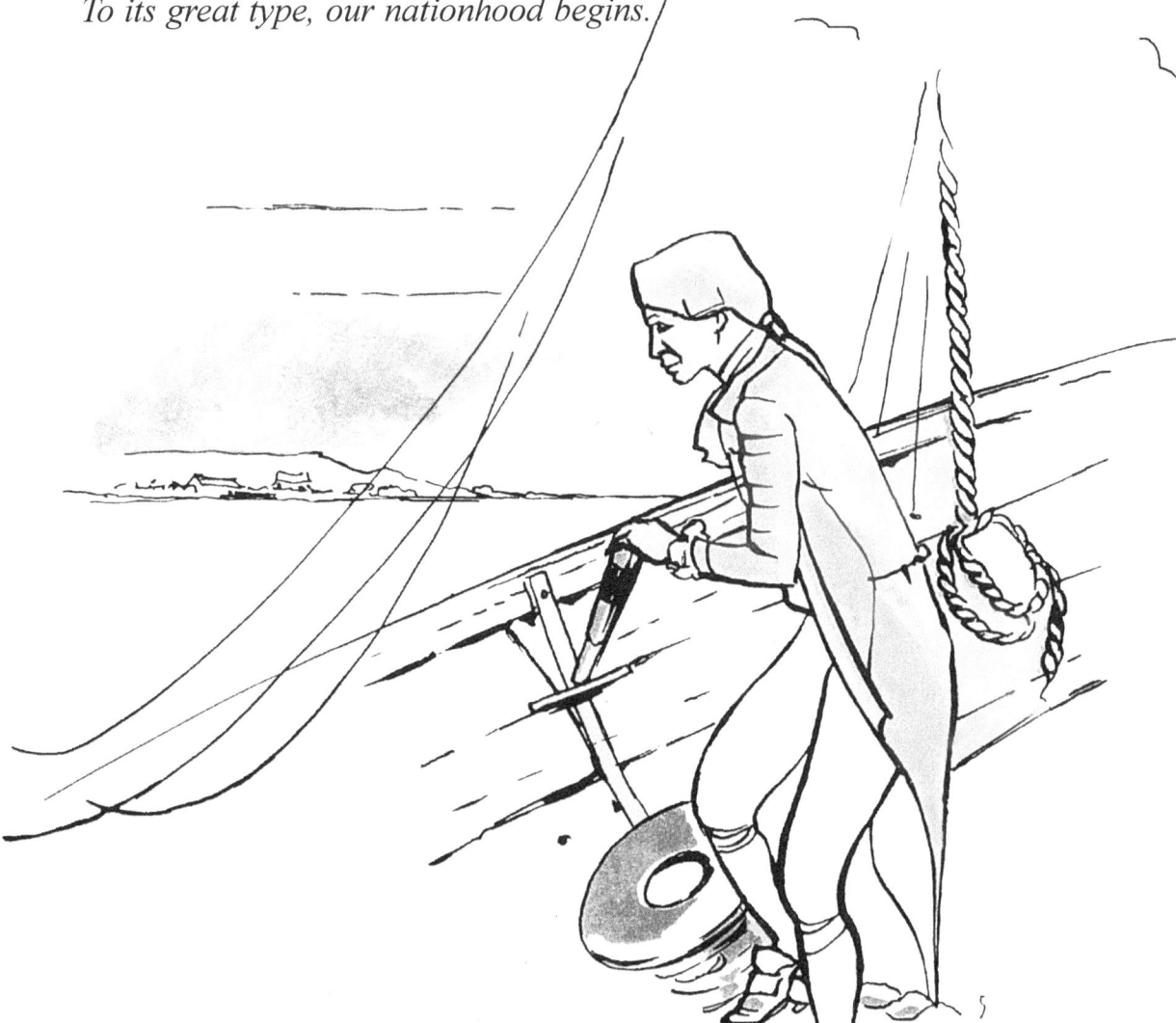

Chapter Four
Rum and Rebellion

THE settlement which Arthur Phillip had begun so well was to continue to grow and prosper, but not before a number of dark, troublesome years had passed and some of the free settlers, marines and redcoats had caused a great deal of trouble. These people were often referred to as "Exclusionists" as they argued that all convicts and even those who had served their time as convicts ("emancipists") should be excluded from all social life in the colony.

You will remember that the marines who came out with the first fleet disliked guarding the convicts at labour. They felt their work was simply to shoulder their guns and to be ready to fight in defence of the colony should the need ever arise. Now this was unfortunate, because Phillip certainly needed *somebody* to supervise each group of convicts — someone who would make sure the convicts *did* the work they were sent to do without trying to escape, or hide, or destroy the tools. When the marines refused to carry out this duty, Phillip decided to do two things: to ask for a regiment of men who would carry out the work and, secondly, to appoint some of the more trustworthy convicts as overseers in charge of work groups.

In answer to Phillip's request a special regiment of soldiers, to be known as the *New South Wales Corps*, was sent to Sydney Cove. These men served Phillip until he returned to England. When he did leave the colony he was not replaced for two long years, and the commander of the regiment, the Lieutenant-Governor, became the ruler of the colony.

It was unfortunate that Lieutenant-Governor Grose took several actions which were to cause trouble for many years to come. He swept away many of Phillip's wise plans for the building of the town of Sydney. Phillip wanted a model town to grow up, with fine buildings and good, straight streets at least 60 metres wide. When Grose put these plans aside, the town grew up in rather a higgledy-piggledy fashion, with narrow, criss-crossing streets and poorly planned buildings. All sorts of future traffic and town-planning problems were to result from this rash mistake made by Grose; but another action of his was to cause even greater trouble in the young colony. He made the mistake of giving his soldier friends so much power that they thought they could do almost whatever they pleased in Sydney Town. One of these men was John Macarthur and he was to be a real troublemaker, making things very difficult for several future governors.

The British Government most unwisely gave Grose approval to give areas of land to the officers and men of the *New South Wales Corps*. Grose made grants of land to his officer friends, and also gave them convict labourers to work their land. When the crops on the officers'

lands were harvested, they were bought by the Government to feed the people of the colony. This plan suited the officers very well. They were required to do very little work, having convict labourers to do it all for them, and they began to grow rich by selling their crops to the Government. Because Grose had determined that he and his men would take over control of the law courts and of the administration of the colony, the *New South Wales Corps* had absolute power

Gradually some of the officers of the Corps and other officials in the settlement decided they could very easily take control of almost all the trade in the colony. In order to do this they would meet each ship carrying goods for sale as soon as it arrived in Sydney Harbour. They would then buy all the goods the ship was carrying for sale. As they were then the only ones with such goods for sale in the colony, they were able to ask other colonists to pay huge prices for them.

There was one item, the officers discovered, for which the people were prepared to pay tremendous prices. That article was rum. The fact that rum was wanted so badly by many of the colonists was to give the traders an idea that led to riches for them, even though it meant ruin for many of the colonists. The traders decided to charter ships

to bring rum to the colony. They would buy all the rum as the ships arrived, and then exchange it for the crops harvested by some of the smaller farmers. When these farmers had drunk the rum, they had nothing left — no crops to sell, no money, and no way of getting any money to buy food and clothing for their families. The only thing for them to do was to sell their farms, which they sometimes did very cheaply. Some of the soldiers and ex-convicts who had received land grants sold out because they wanted to return to England, but many of the smaller farmers foolishly lost all they had worked so hard to get — just for a few litres of rum.

Grose did nothing to stop the officials getting richer. Indeed, he allowed a problem to begin and develop which was to cause great hardship and trouble in the colony.

Both Governor Hunter (1795-1800) and Governor King (1800-1806) tried hard to put an end to the many problems caused by the rum trade, but neither Governor was successful. The power held by the soldiers was too great. They were able to disobey both Governors and also the orders of the British Government, and they continued to trade in rum. They were determined to make fortunes as quickly and as easily as they could, and they intended to let nobody stop them. It seems that the British Government would have been wise to recall the disobedient soldiers to England. Instead of doing this, when King had to be replaced because of his ill health, it was decided to send out a new Governor, who they hoped would be able to defeat the power of the rum-traders. The man they sent would have to be strong, determined and masterful. The Government believed that Captain William Bligh *was* such a man.

Bligh had been captain of a ship called the *Bounty*. After visiting Tahiti, the crew of the *Bounty* had decided to mutiny against Bligh. They had seen the happy, carefree life of the natives on Tahiti, and were determined to go back to the island and live with the natives for the rest of their lives. "Anyway," they reasoned, "this Captain Bligh is a hard, stern man. His rules are strict and his punishments are harsh. Let us put him and his friends into one of the boats and we'll take the *Bounty* back to Tahiti."

With eighteen loyal men Captain Bligh was put into an open boat and set adrift. His boat was only about seven metres long, a little more than two metres broad, and less than a metre deep. The mutineers expected that, in such a small boat, Bligh could do nothing more than land on one of the Pacific islands and settle there. Bligh had different ideas. He at once set out for Timor, knowing that if he could get there he would be able to get a ship to take his men and himself back to England.

For many weeks Bligh steered his boat through dangerous seas, he and the others living on a piece of biscuit each and a little water as the daily ration. At last, after travelling along ocean currents for nearly 5800 kilometres, the little boat bobbed its way safely to Timor.

On his return to England Captain Bligh was greeted as a magnificent sailor and a courageous leader of men, and when a strong, determined Governor was needed for New South Wales it was no surprise that Captain William Bligh was chosen for the job.

So determined was Bligh to defeat the rum trade in New South Wales, and at the same time to weaken the power the officials and traders had obtained for themselves, that the traders soon decided they must choose between two courses of action — either they must give in to Bligh, or they must rise in force against the Governor. They chose to rebel.

Following a serious argument with John Macarthur, Bligh decided to have Macarthur thrown into prison. Many people considered that Macarthur deserved to be in prison but his friends in the New South Wales Corps and other members of the more privileged classes (especially the Exclusionists) in the colony were determined he should be released, and an excited crowd of his supporters demanded that the Commander of the Corps, Major Johnston, should march his redcoats to Government House, arrest Bligh, and release Macarthur.

Johnston grouped his men together, and along the road to Government House they marched. They seized the Governor, placed him under arrest and marched with him back to the prison.

With Bligh in prison the colony was left without a Governor, so Johnston agreed to assume control until the new Governor was appointed or until the British Government decided what steps would be taken.

At last the authorities in England realized that the trouble-making New South Wales Corps had to be recalled. They decided to send out a completely new regiment — the Seventy-third Regiment of Highlanders. Their leader was Colonel Lachlan Macquarie, and it was finally decided he should also be the Governor of the colony. This meant that the same man was now in charge of both the colony and the soldiers, and that all the people had to obey him. This was a very wise decision. Before long the rum trade was stopped, and a wonderful new period of discovery and settlement began in New South Wales.

Chapter Five
Bass and Flinders Map the Coastline

DURING the years between the departure of Governor Phillip in 1792 and the arrival of Governor Macquarie in 1810 many of the soldiers and officials had been interested in grasping as much for themselves as they possibly could — no matter who was ruined in the taking. The efforts of Governors Hunter, King and Bligh were constantly frustrated by the opposition of such people. However, there were others in the colony who wanted to explore the new land and find answers to some of its mysteries. Two such men were George Bass and Matthew Flinders.

When Matthew Flinders was a boy, he had read a book that thrilled him so much he decided to become a sailor. The book was *Robinson Crusoe* and young Matthew dreamt of the excitement and adventure of life on board a ship. When he was old enough, Matthew made his dream come true. He joined the navy, fought against the French, and sailed the seas in ships both large and small. In 1795, as a midshipman on the *Reliance*, a frigate sent to carry Governor Hunter to New South Wales, Matthew became a close friend of the ship's doctor. You see, Matthew Flinders and surgeon George Bass had two great interests in common. They both loved the sea, and they both wanted to discover and explore new places.

George Bass had brought his own boat with him. It was a tiny boat — less than 2.5 metres long and just 1.5 metres wide — but Bass intended to spend his free time in New South Wales sailing around in this small craft.

Do you remember the little boy in the fairy story who was no bigger than his father's thumb? What do you think Bass had called his tiny boat? Why, he called it the *Tom Thumb*, because it, too, was so very small. It was the type of little boat that most people are happy enough to use on the still waters of a lake, but Bass and Flinders had different plans for it. They decided to use it for trips of exploration along the coastline of New South Wales.

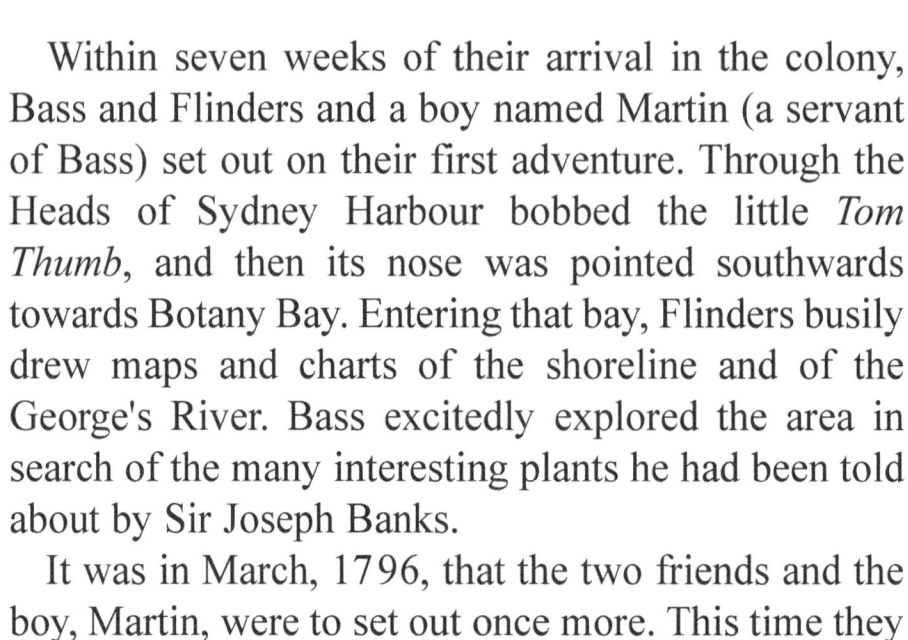

Within seven weeks of their arrival in the colony, Bass and Flinders and a boy named Martin (a servant of Bass) set out on their first adventure. Through the Heads of Sydney Harbour bobbed the little *Tom Thumb*, and then its nose was pointed southwards towards Botany Bay. Entering that bay, Flinders busily drew maps and charts of the shoreline and of the George's River. Bass excitedly explored the area in search of the many interesting plants he had been told about by Sir Joseph Banks.

It was in March, 1796, that the two friends and the boy, Martin, were to set out once more. This time they used a boat which was a little larger than the first *Tom Thumb*, so they called it *Tom Thumb II*. Southward they sailed, until they approached that part of the coast on which Port Kembla is now built. By this time their water barrels were almost empty and they decided to go ashore to look for fresh water.

Everything went well until the little boat was in the surf. Then a huge wave lifted it high into the air, carried it along swiftly towards the beach and dumped it into the shallows. The explorers were soaked and so were all their provisions. They must have looked a sorry sight as they dragged the little boat back to an upright position.

The three friends realized that they were now in great danger. If the natives were to see them, and decide to attack, there was little the explorers could do. In those days guns had to be loaded with a loose black gunpowder, before the shot was put into the gun. This powder had to be carried in special pouches, and the user had to be most careful not to get it wet, for otherwise the powder would not ignite and the gun would not fire. It was therefore very important to find a safe landing-place where they could dry out all their provisions.

After pushing the *Tom Thumb II* back into the surf and rowing through the breakers, the adventurers sailed northwards until an opening in the shoreline was seen. Into the opening they steered and were soon delighted to see it widen out to form a large lake, or lagoon. They were not aware that several pairs of eyes were secretly watching as the little boat crept towards the bank.

On the banks of the lagoon, which they named *Tom Thumb's Lagoon*, the three friends began to spread out their wet clothes, powder and other provisions. Soon they had the feeling that they were not alone on the banks of the lagoon. They had the uneasy feeling that others were watching as they worked. Looking up, they saw a group of twenty or more natives closing in upon them. What were the explorers to do? What would *you* have done? They knew they had no chance of firing their guns if the natives decided to attack. There was also little hope of escaping. Native spears would have brought them down before they could have pushed the *Tom Thumb II* into the water. What *was* to be done?

The explorers were, in fact, to be helped by the click! clip! of a pair of scissors. Flinders, remembering that natives liked shiny things, decided he would try to make friends with them while Bass and Martin dried the supplies. Quickly grabbing the pair of scissors, Flinders showed the natives that the strange, shiny things he held in his hands could be used to cut hair and, yes, beards, too! Before long the natives were squatting down for a haircut and beard trim.

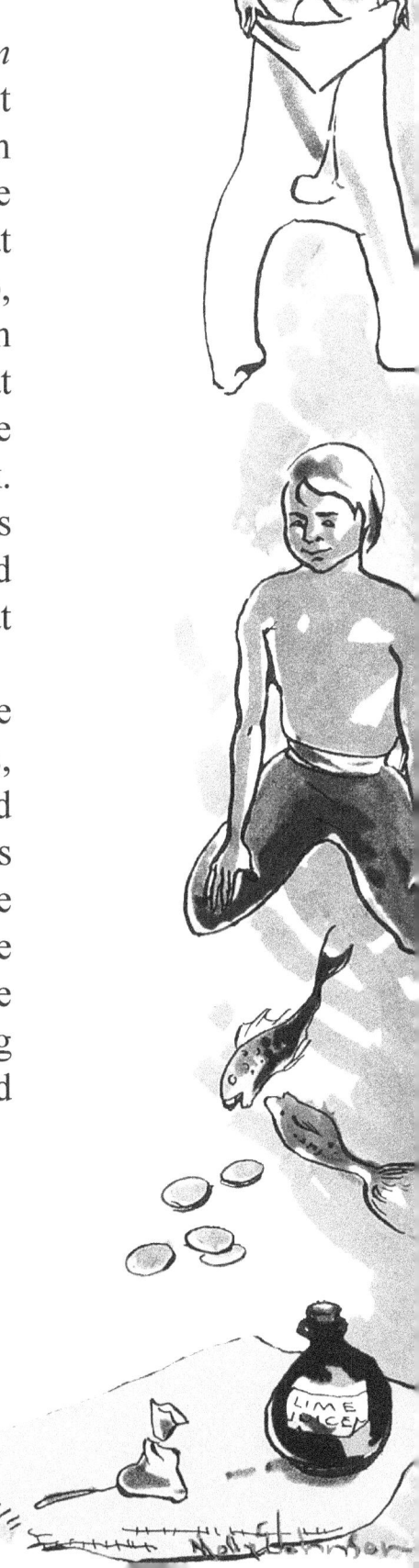

As Flinders was using a large pair of scissors, he was able to act as barber for quite a number of the natives. He later wrote, "The shaving of a dozen or more did not occupy me long." According to the story later written by him, some of the natives thoroughly enjoyed the entertainment but there were a few who were a little frightened of the snip, snip of the blades, especially when the scissors went anywhere near their noses. However, even the frightened ones tried to look brave and pretend that they did not care.

The natives remained friendly until, at last, Bass and the boy, Martin, were able to dry out all the stores. Once again the three friends climbed into the *Tom Thumb II* and moved out towards the open sea, where they began to nose their way northward, back towards Port Jackson. One night they dropped anchor beside a high cliff.

It was about 10 o'clock when the three friends noticed that the boat was beginning to lift and fall on a rising sea. A strong, southerly wind soon commenced to blow, and Bass and Flinders, believing that rough weather was on the way, decided to take up anchor and head for the open sea.

Flinders knew that, if they stayed close to shore, they were in great danger of being smashed against the rocky base of the cliff. There was nothing for it but to head out to sea, and try to ride out the storm.

What a night that was! "The shade of the cliffs over our heads and the noise of the surfs breaking at our feet," Flinders later wrote, "were the directions by which our course was steered parallel to the coast." Bass clung tightly to the sheet of the sail, drawing it in or letting it out, according to the strength of the wind and the size of the sea. Flinders placed an oar over the stern and used it as a rudder to steer the boat, while the boy, Martin, was kept busy baling out. Only by excellent seamanship did the explorers escape disaster in the fury of that sea. "A single wrong movement, or a moment's inattention," wrote Flinders, "would have sent us to the bottom."

You can be certain that Bass and Flinders were greatly relieved when they saw, to their left, a long line of breakers. This told them there would be a break in the line of cliffs and an opening of some sort — a beach, or a bay, or a cove — beyond the line of breakers. The explorers decided to take down the sail, ship the mast, and row hard for the shore. Very soon they had safely arrived in a little sheltered cove.

The place where *Tom Thumb II* had landed was known by the aboriginal name of Watta Mowlee or Wattamolla. The three adventurers decided to call the place of refuge *Providential Cove*, because it had given them shelter on that dreadful night. Today, at Wattamolla, a memorial to the explorers reads:

<blockquote>
WATTAMOLLA
(Watta Mowlee)
Matthew Flinders, George Bass and the
Boy Martin in the boat "Tom Thumb"
Took refuge in this bay named by them
Providential Cove, March 1796.
</blockquote>

The explorers spent the night in Providential Cove and set out the next day to continue their journey towards Port Jackson. The seas had calmed and good progress was made. *Tom Thumb II* rode smoothly through the ocean until a wide opening in the coastline was seen. Bass and Flinders were excited to find a harbour, and they named it *Port Hacking*. They spent the rest of that day exploring the shores of this port.

On the evening of the next day the tired little boat and three exhausted, but happy explorers completed their journey. The Tom Thumb II nosed through the Heads, bobbing up and down on the swell and making her way steadily for Sydney Cove. When at last she was safely tied up, the three contented members of the crew stepped ashore and looked back at her. She looked just like any other tiny boat in the harbour, but how much more adventure had she experienced!

Flinders and Bass did not sail together again until 1798. Bass, in 1797, made two trips in whale-boats. In the first of these he sailed about fifty kilometres south of Botany Bay, and there discovered a seam of coal, about two metres thick, which came right through to show in the face of the cliff. Bass called the place Coalcliff and took three bags of the coal back to Port Jackson. It was found to be good coal which would burn well to give great heat. Actually Bass had discovered something very important, for the seam of coal which he found continues under the ground all the way from Coalcliff to Lithgow and Maitland. Later it was to play an important part in the industries of New South Wales. A few weeks after this, John Shortland discovered coal near the mouth of a river which he called the *Hunter*, in honour of the Governor. Today the city of Newcastle is built at the mouth of the *Hunter*, and coal from the Newcastle area was used for many years in the giant blast furnaces and open-hearth furnaces of the Newcastle steel-works. Today the coal from this and other seams is one of Australia's major exports.

Bass's second whale-boat trip took him past the Shoalhaven River, Tuross Lake, Twofold Bay, the Ninety-Mile Beach, Wilson's Promontory and Western Port. All of these were discovered and named by Bass. At the same time, of course, he became the first European to sail through that stormy, windswept stretch of water now known as *Bass Strait*, which separates Tasmania from the mainland of Australia.

Although he had sailed through the strait between Tasmania and the mainland, Bass could not be absolutely certain that there actually was a strait. You see, he had not *seen* Tasmania and therefore could not be completely certain that Tasmania was not joined to the mainland. In 1798 he and Flinders again joined forces, so that they could find out for certain whether or not Tasmania was an island.

In a little sloop called the *Norfolk*, Bass and Flinders were able to circumnavigate (or sail around) Tasmania. They thus proved it to be an island, and at the same time mapped the coastline.

While at anchor in the Derwent River, on which Hobart now stands, Bass was most impressed by the mountain which seemed to rise almost from the very edge of the water and then to soar to a height of some 1220 metres. Of course there are many mountains much higher than that, but this one seems particularly grand as it is so close to the coast. Bass made up his mind to climb to the summit. With his two dogs he set out, and toiled up the long, steep grade until he was able to stand on the top. Once there, Bass was able to see a magnificent view which tourists travel many kilometres to see today. Far below him, to the east and south, stretched the ocean and the rugged outline of the coast, while to the north and west were the tree-covered summits and slopes of other mountains. Before leaving the Derwent Bass and Flinders named the mountain *Mount Wellington*.

Careful notes and sketches were made by Bass whenever he had the opportunity of observing an animal, bird or plant in Tasmania. While he did this, Flinders busied himself mapping the coastline on his charts. Inlets, bays, rivers, points, peninsulas, and ports were all carefully drawn. On his maps he placed the names of *Port Dalrymple* and the *Tamar River*, *Cape Grim*, *Mount Heemskirk* and *Mount Zeehan* (after Tasman's ships), *South West Cape*, *Storm Bay*, the *Derwent River*, and *Mount Wellington*. Then the *Norfolk* headed for home, arriving at Port Jackson in January, 1799.

The trip in the *Norfolk* was the last Bass and Flinders were to make together, but in 1801-1803 Flinders was to make yet another voyage of importance to Australia.

Although much of the coastline of Australia and Tasmania had been charted by this time, there were still some parts which had not been explored. Flinders decided to attempt a voyage that would give the answers to any questions still remaining concerning the mainland coastline. This voyage was to be a trip right around Australia. Sir Joseph Banks considered this voyage necessary and gave his support to Flinders. Finally the British Government put the *Investigator*, a ship of 300 tonnes, under Flinders' command and gave him the task of exploring the coasts of *Terra Australis* (the early name given to Australia).

Some of the stores taken aboard the *Investigator* before the voyage began would have surprised most people. There were 500 pocket-knives taken below, as well as 500 looking-glasses, 100 combs, coloured cloth, axes, hatchets, medals and new coins. Can you guess why these things were taken on the voyage? That's right. The bright, colourful things and useful implements such as knives and axes, were later to be given as presents to the Aboriginals, in order to win their friendship and trust.

Having travelled from England around the Cape of Good Hope, Flinders at last sighted Cape Leeuwin — the little cape in the southwestern corner of Australia. From this point Flinders began to draw his charts. He sailed the whole length of the Great Australian Bight and

then into both Spencer's Gulf and Saint Vincent's Gulf. When he found they were both gulfs and not channels cutting Australia in two, as some people thought, he had solved yet another mystery. From there he discovered Kangaroo Island and then went on to Encounter Bay. There, on the 8th April, 1802, Flinders was surprised to see other ships in the bay. They were French ships and were under the command of Baudin. He had been sent to lead a scientific expedition. The two explorers had friendly discussions, comparing notes on the places each had visited. When they parted, Baudin sailed toward the west and Flinders to the east, continuing on to Port Jackson.

This visit by Baudin, and others by Frenchmen to our coasts, made the British authorities wonder whether the French intended making settlements on the Australian mainland. Their concern about this possibility was one of the reasons for other British settlements being made.

At Port Jackson the *Investigator* was refitted, and then she set out in a northerly direction on a voyage that was to take her around Australia. It was to be many months before she was to re-enter Port Jackson, and the sailors and the famous navigator were perhaps a little lucky to return at all because, in Flinders' own words, the *Investigator* was by then "worn-out and dangerous, decayed both in skin and bone". Did you know that Flinders had sailed with a very special friend on board? In Macquarie Street, Sydney, there is a statue of Flinders and behind

him is also a statue of his much-loved companion — who is curled up comfortably on a window-sill of the Public Library! It is a statue of "Trim", the cat!

Thanks especially to the work of Flinders but also to navigators from several other nations, the whole of the coastline of Terra Australis had now been charted. People now knew for certain the *shape* of the land. What they did not know and had yet to discover was the type of country that lay *inside* that shape.

The story of the exploration of Australia's inland is really a story of many men. It is the story of those who were challenged by a mystery and decided to take up the challenge. In this book there will not be the space to tell of the deeds of all these men, but those who finally solved the great mysteries of the inland are included.

What *were* some of these great mysteries? People were curious to know just what lay beyond the range of mountains to the west of Sydney. They wanted to know what sort of country lay along the coast to the north of Sydney. That was another problem to be solved. A third problem was how to discover what sort of country lay between Sydney and Western Port, and whether or not settlements could be made on that land.

We shall see in the next chapter that as some of these problems were solved, they automatically made others. For example, when the mystery of the range of mountains to the west of Sydney was finally solved, a number of rivers were discovered. The question then was asked, "Where do these rivers flow? Do they end in a desert, or perhaps in an inland sea? Do they finally flow into the sea somewhere?" The white men did not know the answers to such problems, but we are now going to read the stories of some of the men who were determined to find out.

Chapter Six
Over the Barrier

GOVERNOR Lachlan Macquarie arrived in the colony at the very end of 1809. He ruled the colony for twelve years, and during that time there was an exciting development of the colony. Macquarie helped all people who he believed were making a worth-while effort in the colony. He helped the emancipists (convicts who had served their time), including Dr. William Redfern, the architect Francis Greenway and the businessman Simeon Lord. He encouraged small landholders and he gave his interested support to the men who wanted to explore the country.

It was indeed unfortunate that rich "exclusionists", like the wealthy Rev. Samuel Marsden and, later, John Macarthur, (who had been granted large areas of land for development of the wool and mutton industries) and others of the rich and privileged classes were so determined to oppose Macquarie's efforts to improve the lives of the emancipists.

Macquarie was keen to know just what sort of country existed on the other side of the mountain range to the west of Sydney. Those who had tried to conquer this barrier had begun by following one of the valleys, hoping they would be able to find a pass *through* the ranges rather than go over them. These men were all to be disappointed, as sooner or later the valleys seemed to end in steep, rugged cliffs over which the explorers could not climb.

By the year 1813 it became very important that a way over the ranges be found. Most of the good, fertile country between Sydney and the mountains had by then been occupied, and farmers were needing more land for their growing herds of cattle and flocks of sheep.

Something just had to be done and Gregory Blaxland, a farmer, decided that he would be the man to do it.

Blaxland gathered all the knowledge he could about the mountains *before* attempting to cross them, making several short trips into the foothills to study the type of country through which he would pass. He was lucky enough to meet a kangaroo hunter from the mountains who told Blaxland that it would be possible to go at least some of the way by following the *ridges* instead of the valleys. Blaxland decided to follow this advice and try to climb over the mountains instead of attempting to go through the valleys.

Two other men, Lieutenant William Lawson and William Charles Wentworth, were invited by Blaxland to accompany him on this adventure. Both agreed to go and, with four servants, five dogs, and four pack-horses, they set out from Blaxland's farm on the 11th May, 1813. With them they carried the good wishes of Governor Macquarie and the hopes of the entire colony.

After crossing the Nepean River, the explorers did not progress very far before finding they had tackled no easy task. The journey over the mountains was to be no picnic. In many places there were thickly forested slopes, and in others the ground was covered with a dense, heavy scrub. Often it seemed that the easiest way would have been to descend to the valleys, but, no matter how tough the going on the ridges, Blaxland was determined not to go down into the valleys. Too many others had tried that method and had failed. Blaxland knew that he must stick to the ridges if he were to succeed.

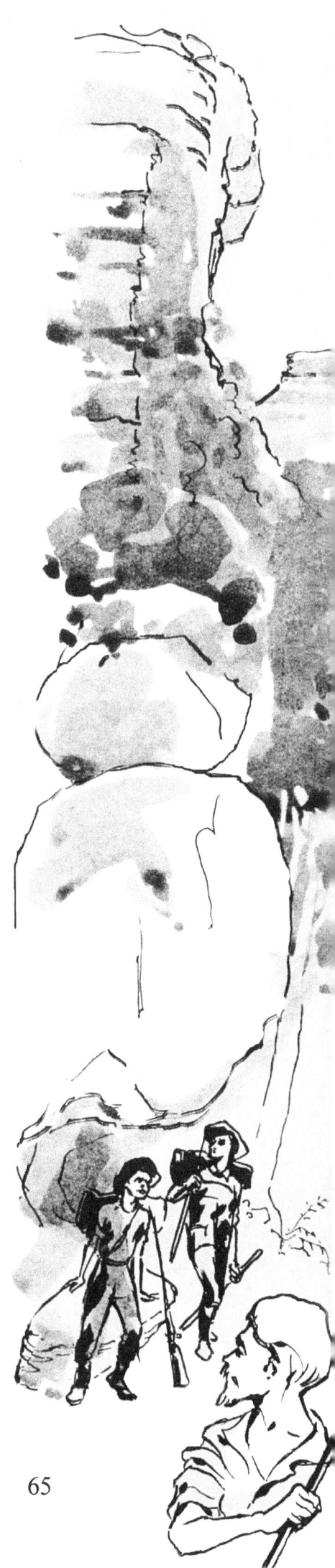

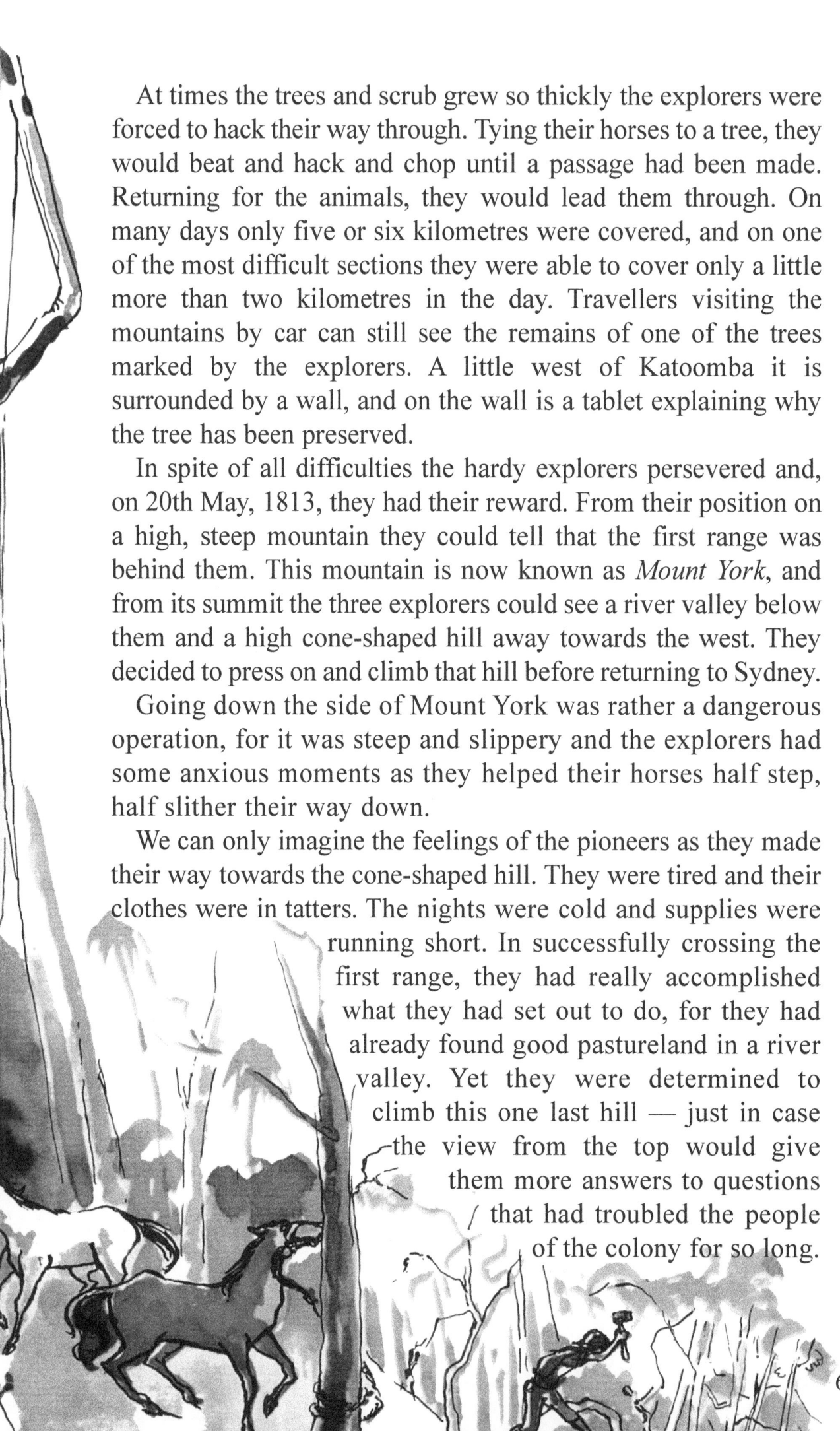

At times the trees and scrub grew so thickly the explorers were forced to hack their way through. Tying their horses to a tree, they would beat and hack and chop until a passage had been made. Returning for the animals, they would lead them through. On many days only five or six kilometres were covered, and on one of the most difficult sections they were able to cover only a little more than two kilometres in the day. Travellers visiting the mountains by car can still see the remains of one of the trees marked by the explorers. A little west of Katoomba it is surrounded by a wall, and on the wall is a tablet explaining why the tree has been preserved.

In spite of all difficulties the hardy explorers persevered and, on 20th May, 1813, they had their reward. From their position on a high, steep mountain they could tell that the first range was behind them. This mountain is now known as *Mount York*, and from its summit the three explorers could see a river valley below them and a high cone-shaped hill away towards the west. They decided to press on and climb that hill before returning to Sydney.

Going down the side of Mount York was rather a dangerous operation, for it was steep and slippery and the explorers had some anxious moments as they helped their horses half step, half slither their way down.

We can only imagine the feelings of the pioneers as they made their way towards the cone-shaped hill. They were tired and their clothes were in tatters. The nights were cold and supplies were running short. In successfully crossing the first range, they had really accomplished what they had set out to do, for they had already found good pastureland in a river valley. Yet they were determined to climb this one last hill — just in case the view from the top would give them more answers to questions that had troubled the people of the colony for so long.

Even though they were weary and footsore, the three explorers scrambled excitedly up the slopes of the high hill. When they were at last on the top, how glad they were that they had made the effort! There, spreading out before them, was a magnificent scene of rich, green grazing land. The men stood and stared. This was indeed a wonderful discovery, and it would be great news to carry back to the people of Sydney. "There is enough grassland here to support the colony for the next thirty years!" exclaimed Blaxland, and the others agreed that the scene from the high hill was indeed a thrilling one.

The explorers were now satisfied. They had crossed the first range of the Great Divide, and they had found excellent pastureland. Now all that remained for them to do was to return to Sydney with the news.

The return journey was difficult, for the men were tired and were running short of food. To make matters worse, they had not marked trees for the first few kilometres of their journey, and they had trouble finding their way home. You can be sure they were relieved and happy when they finally saw familiar landmarks to guide them home.

When the three exhausted, but happy explorers returned to Sydney, the news they carried greatly excited all people in the town. In particular, Governor Macquarie was thrilled with the report of the good pastureland, and he decided to send out a surveyor named George Evans, to follow where the three pioneers had blazed the trail.

It was obvious that good pastures were useless unless the sheep and cattle were able to reach them. A road was necessary, so Evans was asked to plot the route for one. Evans was able fairly easily to follow the trail cut by Blaxland, Wentworth and Lawson and, when he came eventually to the sugar-loaf hill, he named it *Mount Blaxland* to honour the man whose party had finally overcome the mountain barrier and opened the way to the west.

From Mount Blaxland, Evans continued on, feeling that the road he was plotting should end at a site upon which a new settlement could be made. He crossed a stream that was teeming with fish, called it the *Fish River*, and then followed it until it joined with a larger river which flowed away to the west. Evans named this new river the *Macquarie*, and decided that the banks of such a river would be an ideal place for a settlement. Not only was there a plentiful supply of fresh water, but the plains beyond the river were covered with thick, long grass. Evans named these the *Bathurst Plains* and turned to make his way back to Sydney.

Macquarie was thrilled with the news brought back by Evans, and he determined that a road should be built as soon as possible. William Cox, a farmer, was placed in charge of this tremendous task, and he was given a band of thirty men to help him. Most of these men were convicts, but they worked with a will, because they were promised their freedom if the job were done quickly and well.

The work was hard, and neither the mountains nor the weather was on the side of the road-builders. It was winter when they began, and often the weather was cold and wet, but the men worked on, whenever it was possible. Through the valleys and over the ranges could be heard the clang of sledge-hammers, the blast of gunpowder, the ring of axes on timber, and the shouts of men's voices as workers strained against a tree-trunk or heaved as one man to push great boulders out of the way. For six months the work continued and, at the end of that time, a road 162 kilometres long had been constructed.

It was 25th April, 1815, when Governor Macquarie and a party including William Cox, John Oxley, George Evans, Mrs. Macquarie and others, set out to travel the road built by Cox and his men. The coach journey took ten days and, when it was over, Macquarie and the others felt that a little celebration was in order. The flag was hoisted, three volleys were fired, cheers rang out, the Governor made a little speech and then gave the name "*Bathurst*" to the site on which they were standing. Today, in William Street, Bathurst, there is a cairn (a monument of stones) in memory of the event about which you have just read.

Do you remember that Governor Phillip had fine plans for broad streets and well-constructed buildings, but that these plans were swept away when Phillip left the colony? It was a fortunate thing for Sydney that Governor Macquarie was also a man of vision. He is often called "the building Governor", because it was under his instructions that many of Sydney's most handsome structures were planned and built.

Macquarie was determined to bring some order to a higgledy-piggledy settlement, and he found just the right man to help him do it. That man was Francis Greenway. Now Greenway was a convict, but he was also a fine architect. He came from Bath in England and had been known to Phillip who had also lived there. It is probable that Phillip had recommended him to Macquarie. Macquarie was happy to employ him to plan buildings, many of which people still admire for their beauty and strength of design.

Among the Greenway-designed buildings still standing today are the Conservatorium of Music (built originally as the Government House stables); St Matthew's Church at Windsor; St Luke's Church at Liverpool and Hyde Park Barracks (now used as the Law Courts).

Chapter Seven
The Riddle of the Rivers

MACQUARIE was determined to see progress in the colony continue, and so he asked Evans to explore farther towards the west. We can imagine he may have said to Evans, "This river to which you have given my name is indeed a fine stream. I am curious to know where it has its mouth. Mr Evans, I would be obliged if you would undertake to follow this noble stream to its end."

It was, however, to be many years before an answer to the riddle, "To where do these western rivers flow?" could be given.

Although Evans was not able to follow the Macquarie to its mouth, he did find more vast stretches of fine grazing country and still another westward-flowing river. As 1814 was not a good season the river was almost dry, but Evans could see that it would be a large river in a better season, for its banks were wide apart. He named the stream the *Lachlan*, and returned to Bathurst.

Macquarie was pleased to learn that Evans had discovered still more good grazing country and yet another river, but Evans had not solved the problem of these rivers. He had not traced one to its mouth. Macquarie therefore asked John Oxley, the Surveyor-General of the colony, to trace the Lachlan.

It was 1817 when Oxley set out. Evans was second in command. For many kilometres the party followed the Lachlan. There had been good rains that year and the river was wide and fast-flowing. Then bad luck struck. The river seemed to disappear into an extensive, reed-covered swamp. Oxley decided to strike out across country, away from the river. The party began to travel in a south-westerly direction, but, before they had covered many kilometres, the weather became hot and dry and the land was parched, scrubby and useless. It was obvious to Oxley that the expedition must return to the Lachlan.

To their great surprise, the explorers, upon again reaching the Lachlan, found that it had worked its way right through the swamps and was once more a steady stream. Before long, however, swamps were again blocking their path.

How unlucky was poor Oxley! Had he been able to continue for just a few more kilometres along the Lachlan, he would have come to the place where it met the Murrumbidgee. Perhaps he would then have been able to continue along the Murrumbidgee and the Murray, solving the problem of the western rivers. But this was not to be. Oxley was close to the answer, but the Lachlan swamps finally made him turn and strike out for the Macquarie, which he intended to follow back to Bathurst.

As the explorers neared the Macquarie River, they came to a beautiful area of rolling, grass-covered hills. Flowering shrubs and wattles were in full bloom and there were many grand cypress pine and hardwood trees. The expedition followed one particularly lovely valley which had rich soil and a luxuriant growth of grass. Oxley called this valley the *Wellington Vale*. Through the valley ran a creek which Oxley named the *Bell Creek* and, by following it, the explorers were led back to the Macquarie.

Oxley was not content to leave the problem of the western rivers unanswered, and so in 1818 he set out once more — this time to follow the Macquarie River.

For about 210 kilometres all went well, and then Oxley was to be disappointed by his old enemy, the swamps. However, he was determined to do all in his power to defeat the problem and so he split his party. We can imagine him saying to Evans:

"It seems we are to be plagued forever by these cursed swamps. Therefore it is my opinion that we make a determined effort to beat them here and now. I shall take a party of men in the boat, and see if we are able to find a way through these reeds. I think you should see if you can find a way *around* them. We shall make our base camp here and return to decide which route should be taken by the whole of the party."

So Evans went off in a north-westerly direction, while Oxley tried to battle through the swamps. They seemed to spread wider and wider, while in places the reeds reached a height of two metres or more.

Wisely, he decided to return to the main camp before becoming hopelessly lost in the jungle of reeds.

When Evans reached the camp, he was not able to report a way around the swamps either, but he was able to give Oxley some good news. He had discovered yet another river. This time it was the one we now call the *Castlereagh*. It did not take Oxley long to strike out for this new river, leaving the Macquarie to the huge, annoying marshes that seemed to swallow it up. Today we know this area as the *Macquarie Marshes*, a very important wetlands area, habitat for many waterbirds.

The rest of Oxley's trip was much more rewarding. He crossed the Castlereagh, and discovered the *Warrumbungle Range*, a group of rugged peaks rising sharply and unexpectedly from the plain. These peaks are densely covered with beautiful native flora. He skirted around it to come to a glorious area of rich pastureland. He called this area the *Liverpool Plains*. After discovering the *Peel River*, the expedition set out for the Great Dividing Range. Oxley intended to cross the mountains and head for the coast, which he would follow back to Sydney.

After climbing the western slopes of the Dividing Range and so reaching its top, the men scrambled to the peak of one especially high mountain. From the summit they were able to look out upon the Pacific Ocean and, because of this, Oxley called the mountain *Mount Seaview*.

The eastern slopes of the Dividing Range are much steeper than the gradual western slopes. The men had to climb, slip, slide and stumble until, at last, they were on the coastal plains.

After discovering the *Hastings River* and tracing its course to the coast, the explorers then set out for Port Stephens. Many were the streamlets and creeks to be crossed and weary were the men, but the end was in sight now and the explorers pressed on bravely. Then something happened to make them constantly fear for their lives.

There was a silent movement in the bushes; a rushing, swishing sound in the air; a dull thud and a scream from one of the men. This was the warning! Hostile Aboriginals were close by. The man was not killed, but he was badly injured and had to be carried from that point.

The boat had been left on the other side of the mountains, for it would have been too cumbersome to haul across. However, they now missed this piece of equipment very greatly. It seems, therefore, that Fate decided to smile upon the weary little band for, as they toiled doggedly along the coast one day, they saw something sticking up through the sand on the beach. Upon examination they found the object to be an old ship's boat, apparently washed up during a storm. It was very much in need of repair, but at least it *was* a boat and it helped them to cross the remaining streams until Port Stephens was finally reached. There the injured servant was given proper attention, and the party of explorers was able to board a ship to take them to Sydney. A journey which had taken the expedition over many hundreds of kilometres was over at last.

Although Oxley had not solved the riddle of the western rivers, his two journeys certainly did answer some other problems. He had proved that there were other important rivers, some flowing westward and others eastward from their sources in the Great Dividing Range. He had further discovered that there was valuable grazing land in the inland, particularly in that area which he called the Liverpool Plains.

Of course it was one thing for Oxley to return with the news of rich, verdant pastures, but it was quite another to explain how the Liverpool plains could be reached. Farmers were not prepared to take their stock on the long journey from the Bathurst plains and *around* the Warrumbungle mountains. If only a way *through* the mountains could be found!

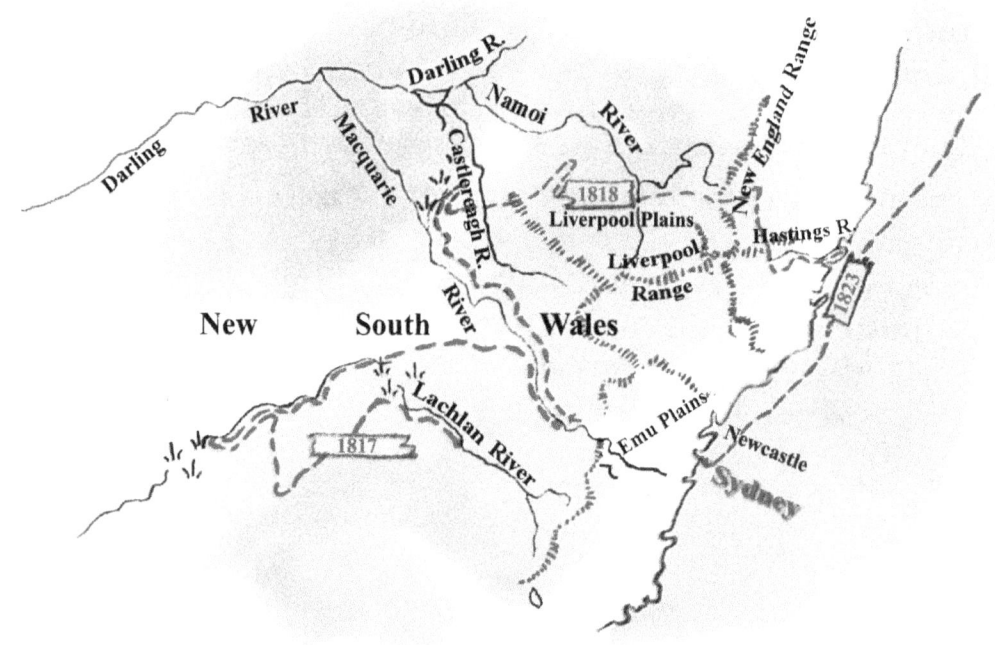

Have you ever heard of Pandora? In Greek mythology Pandora was supposed to carry a special box containing good and wonderful gifts. When she opened the box all these gifts escaped, except *Hope*. There is a pass through the Warrumbungle mountains named Pandora's Pass, because Allan Cunningham, the explorer who discovered it in 1823, felt that it would give *hope* to the men who wanted to take their sheep and cattle to the rich Liverpool plains.

The year 1823 was important for still another discovery and, once more, Oxley was involved. The new Governor of the colony was Sir Thomas Brisbane. He thought that another convict settlement should be established some distance from Sydney, and so he sent Oxley north in a boat to look for a suitable site.

One evening, after anchoring the *Mermaid* a short distance from the shore, Oxley was surprised to see a number of Aborigines running down the beach. They were waving their hands excitedly and calling out to the men in the boat. Now this was strange enough, but it was indeed amazing for Oxley to hear English words being shouted by one of the "natives". Some of the men were ordered to row Oxley ashore, so that he could discover just how this "Aborigine" was able to speak such fluent English.

As the boat approached the shore, Oxley discovered the answer to his little problem. The English voice actually belonged to an *English man*! We can just imagine the conversation that took place:

"Well, sir," Oxley began as he leapt ashore, "would you be so good as to explain your presence here? I cannot understand anyone living such a primitive life by choice."

"My name be Tom Pamphlett, Sir. There were three others with me at first. In an open boat we left Sydney to look for good cedar along the coast. We were driven south by a gale. After the gale was over, we began to sail north towards Botany Bay. Bad luck we had, though, Sir. Our boat was wrecked in another storm and we were cast up on the shore. That is, three of us were. The other died of thirst while we were at sea. A dreadful time we had, Sir, to be sure, and we were afraid we would be killed by the natives. But, instead of killing us, these natives have been very good to us all, keeping the three of us alive."

"Then the other two are also here with the natives?" the astonished Oxley inquired.

"Well, no, Sir," Pamphlett continued. "You see, Sir, Parsons, one of the others, has walked off to the north, looking for Sydney. But the other one, Finnegan be his name, Sir, is living here with the natives and me. I do hope Parsons gets to Sydney safely."

"I can assure you, my man," replied Oxley, "that Parsons has no hope of reaching Sydney safely if he is walking northwards from here. We are *already* north of Sydney."

"But when we began from Sydney we were headed *south* in our boat," protested Pamphlett.

"Then you must have been turned around by the gale. I must say, Pamphlett, that your story has some unlikely points about it. You are not, by any chance, escaped convicts?"

"Convicts? No, Sir!" exclaimed Pamphlett. "Honest men we be, and true, Sir. Else, why would I be asking you to take Finnegan and m'self back to Sydney?"

"True, true," Oxley agreed. "Well, I shall help you if I can. In the meantime I should introduce myself. My name is Oxley and, as Surveyor-General of this colony, it is my duty to look for a suitable place for a new convict settlement."

"Then we can help one another," replied Pamphlett. "If you will come with Finnegan and m'self, we can show you just the spot for a settlement."

Pamphlett was as good as his word. He and Finnegan took Oxley back along the coast until they reached the mouth of a fine stream. Oxley agreed that this would be an ideal place for the settlement, and he named the new river the Brisbane after the Governor. It was time, then, for the party to head back for Sydney.

The prison camp was established in the next year. Oxley and Cunningham both went along. Oxley was there to show the way, while Cunningham wanted to see if he could find any new plants, for he was a keen botanist. The camp was finally set at the site of the present city of Brisbane, capital of Queensland. I suppose you can guess that Oxley wanted to do something else? Why, of course! He went back to

visit the tribe of natives who had helped Pamphlett and Finnegan. Oxley wanted to ask them if Parsons had returned, or if any of their friends had reported seeing anything of him. Imagine Oxley's surprise and pleasure when Parsons himself was there to welcome him! Parsons explained that the farther north he had walked, the *hotter* it had become, until at last he was convinced that he was walking away from rather than towards Sydney. You can be sure that Parsons was glad to see Oxley and to be taken home by ship to Port Jackson.

Thanks to the work of Blaxland, Evans, Oxley, Cunningham and others, the areas to the west and north of Sydney had been fairly well explored by the year 1824. Governor Brisbane now wished to know what sort of country lay to the south of the settlement — that is, the country between Port Jackson and Bass Strait. Two men were chosen to lead a party of exploration over this land and to make their report to Governor Brisbane. One of these men was William Hovell, a retired English Sea Captain, while the other was Hamilton Hume, an Australian-born farmer who owned land at both Appin and Lake George. Hume was an excellent choice. He was strong, fearless and a most experienced bushman. Hovell, however, was a headstrong man who knew little of the Australian bush but who offered to help to pay for the expedition on the condition he could be the joint leader. Several times Hovell was to make a nuisance of himself on the trip by opposing decisions made by Hume.

It was 3rd October, 1824, when Hume and Hovell set out from Appin with two bullock drays, six convict workers, horses and stores. After a journey of five days they came to a homestead near the shores of Lake George. This was the home of Hume's sister, Mary, and her husband.

For several days the explorers rested at Mary's home and then, with Mary's good wishes ringing in their ears, they set off once more. Two days later they stopped at Hume's own property at Lake George. Here they made a final check of equipment, and then they set out into the unknown.

Can you imagine how the explorers felt as they trod forward? Hume was a fine bushman, and he was confident of his own ability to lead the little group. He was probably just a little worried that Hovell would try to rely too much on the instruments he carried rather than upon Hume's experience.

The explorers enjoyed easy travel until, on the third day, they came upon rough, stony country. It was on the afternoon of the same day that they met their first real obstacle. Quite unexpectedly the swollen waters of the Murrumbidgee River appeared in front of them. They made camp and waited for a couple of days, hoping for the waters to subside. Once again, as we know what each of the men was like, we can imagine the conversation taking place: "It's still a banker," said Hume at last. "I'm afraid we'll have some trouble getting over."

"Getting over?" asked Hovell. "Surely you don't intend trying to cross that river, Hume. Why, it's in flood! We'd never find a place shallow enough to ford it, and how else can a river be crossed without a bridge or a boat?"

"Perhaps we could *make* a boat," answered Hume. He removed the wheels from one of the drays, wrapped a tarpaulin firmly around the bottom and sides, and then tied the tarpaulin securely to each of the four corners. This made a waterproof, flat-bottomed boat, but, of course, this wasn't enough, as such a boat would be swept away in a stream moving as swiftly as the Murrumbidgee was at that moment.

"There is only one thing to do," declared Hume. "One of the other men shall swim with me to the other bank. We shall carry a light line between us. Another light line shall be tied to the centre of the first, and one man on this side shall gradually pay it out as we swim across. When we are safely over, he must then tie a heavier line to the end of the light one. We'll pull one end of the heavy line across. This heavy line is to be very securely tied to trees on both sides of the river. Using this rope, we can ferry the boat across the river. Now, who's coming with me?"

"I'll come," answered Tom Boyd, one of the convict helpers.

"Good man, Tom. Let's get ready."

The swim across was extremely dangerous. Both Hume and Boyd were, several times, forced under by the strength of the current and the weight of the line. They were both exhausted when finally they scrambled up the far bank. They pulled the heavy line across and tied it firmly to a tree. This was done on the other side of the river also and then the rest was easy.

Several times the "boat" was pulled back and forth, ferrying men and supplies. The cattle, tied to the back of the punt, were swum across. By evening that day everything was safely on the other side.

As the fire was being lit and preparations for the evening meal were being made, Hovell came up to Hume and said, "Hume, I still feel you took a great risk, but I admire you for it."

"Thank you, Hovell," answered Hume. "Now I shall tell you a secret. The idea of the punt is not a new one. I have seen bushmen use it before. You know, Hovell, there are not many rivers that can stop a good bushman."

You can be sure that Hamilton Hume slept very soundly that night, for he was happy in the knowledge his bushmanship had led the little group safely through the first dangerous problem.

From this point the country became so rough and stony that the drays could no longer be used. As many of the stores as they could carry were packed onto the backs of the sturdy bullocks and the drays were left behind. Some of the stores also had to be left, but Hume was amazed to see Hovell leave both the tarpaulin and his frying pan behind. These two things were, in Hume's opinion, completely essential.

Two very difficult weeks of mountain-climbing followed. Up hard, rocky slopes and down again into deep, stony valleys went the men. When it was possible to follow a ridge they did so, even though dead timber and thick scrub blocked their way. At last, as they scaled the top of a high ridge, a magnificent sight greeted their eyes. There, in front of them, was a semicircle of high, rugged, snow-capped mountains. The dazzling whiteness of the snow and the rugged grandeur of the mountains held the men spellbound for several minutes. At last the silence was broken. "If we achieve nothing else," said Hovell, "this discovery makes the trip worthwhile."

All agreed that the beauty of these Australian Alps was indeed worth discovering. It is a pity, however, that these very mountains were to cause a heated argument between the two leaders of the expedition. Hume considered that it was useless to try climbing the snow-capped, rugged mountains in front of them, and he wanted to look for a way around them by travelling farther west. Hovell was determined to follow their original plan to go straight ahead. Finally, growing tired of argument, Hume told Hovell to go wherever he pleased, but he, Hume, would look for a way around the mountains.

The leaders decided to take three men each and split up. When the stores were being divided, Hume was furious to see Hovell take one certain article with him. Guess what it was! It was Hume's frying pan! Hume needn't have worried. Before night fell, Hovell realized just how foolish he had been. Without Hume's bushmanship Hovell felt lost and, anyway, those mountains *were* mighty steep and rugged. Hovell retraced his steps and, just as night was falling, he tracked Hume's party to the spot where their camp-fire glowed comfortingly through the stillness.

Toiling on together, the eight men came to the banks of a very broad river. It was 17th November, 1824, and they were standing on the banks of the river we now know as the Murray, on a spot quite near the present city of Albury. Hume called the river the *Hume*, after his father. Although Hovell was later to claim that *he named the river* the Hume after his partner the matter was finally to be of little importance as another explorer (Sturt) re-named it the *Murray*.

Once again Hovell did not want to risk crossing the river. He argued that they should try to trace the *Hume* (now known as the *Murray*) to its mouth. As this would have led them to the junction of the Hume and the Murrumbidgee, then the junction of the Hume and the Darling and finally to the sea, Hovell's suggestion was not a bad one, but it was not in agreement with the instructions they had been given and Hume was determined at least to try to cross the river.

"But there is no possible way of getting the gear across," insisted Hovell. "You have no drays with you now, so you can't make a punt this time."

"It's true that I have no dray, but I can make a punt," replied Hume, and he set about doing it.

First of all, Hume selected six strong saplings. He placed three of them on the ground, a short distance from one another. Across these he placed the other three. After tying the saplings together, Hume had made a a rough raft. Through the framework of this raft he wove strong, but pliable branches of wattle, allowing the wattle to stick out about 30 centimetres all the way round. Hume then very carefully bent

up these extending lengths so that they formed sides. He had made something that looked for all the world like the base and stakes of a huge basket just waiting for someone to weave.

"Now," explained Hume, "this will serve just as well as a dray, once we have tied the tarpaulin firmly under it."

As usual, Hume was right and the group was brought safely to the other side. Thus Hume, Hovell, and the convicts became the first Europeans to set foot into what later became northern Victoria.

Other rivers were discovered on the southward journey. Some of them could be forded, others were crossed by using fallen trees as bridges, and still others had to be crossed in a bushman's punt made by Hume. On several occasions Hovell argued that they should turn back, because supplies were running short. Hume, however, was determined to continue and fortunately had his way.

The explorers had almost reached their goal when they lost the piece of equipment being used to measure the distance travelled each day. It was like a present-day pedometer, with a wheel, axle and handles and a device for indicating the number of revolutions made by the wheel. The explorers called it a "perambulator," but because it was the duty of one of the convicts (Claude Bossawa) to wheel it as they travelled it was nick-named "Claude's Wheelbarrow". The group was on top of a small mountain when Claude lost his grip on the device and it was smashed to bits as it crashed down the mountainside. Of course the explorers named the place *Mount Perambulator*!

The *Mitta Mitta*, the *Kiewa*, the *Ovens* and the *Goulburn* rivers were all discovered and crossed. The Dividing Range of Victoria was reached and climbed, and the rich, rolling, grassy *Iramoo Plains* were discovered. On 16th December, 1824, the exhausted men, their clothes now in tatters and their food supplies running desperately short, came to the end of the journey. They had reached the sea at Corio Bay.

Hume and Hovell thought they had reached Western Port. Instead, they had come to the coast at Port Phillip, near the place where

Geelong stands today. They camped for a day on the shores of the bay and perhaps would have stayed a little longer, except for the fact that a group of natives had chased one of the party. The man's name was Fitzpatrick and he had panicked when the armed natives had appeared. He had tried to shoot at them but his musket had misfired. The angry natives chased him right back to the explorers' camp!

Fortunately Hume kept calm and ordered the members of his party to put their muskets on the ground as a sign they had come in peace. The Aboriginal men were satisfied and finally a friendly meeting took place with the natives becoming highly amused at the way Fitzpatrick had high-tailed it back to camp. However, the ring of smoking camp-fires around the explorers that night looked too much like signal fires for Hume to wish to stay any longer. The next morning found the men up bright and early, packing for the journey home.

The return trip was made a little easier by the fact that some of the rivers, in flood when the explorers had journeyed southwards, had fallen and were much more simple to cross. The party had about one month's rations left and they needed every morsel of that, for it was not until 18th January, 1825, that Hamilton Hume's property at Lake George was reached. It had taken them exactly a month to get home.

Hume and Hovell had answered *one* problem concerning the inland: men now knew what sort of country lay between Lake George and Bass Strait. At the same time, however, they had made another problem even more difficult to answer. They had discovered several new westward-flowing rivers about which people were still to ask, "Where do they flow?"

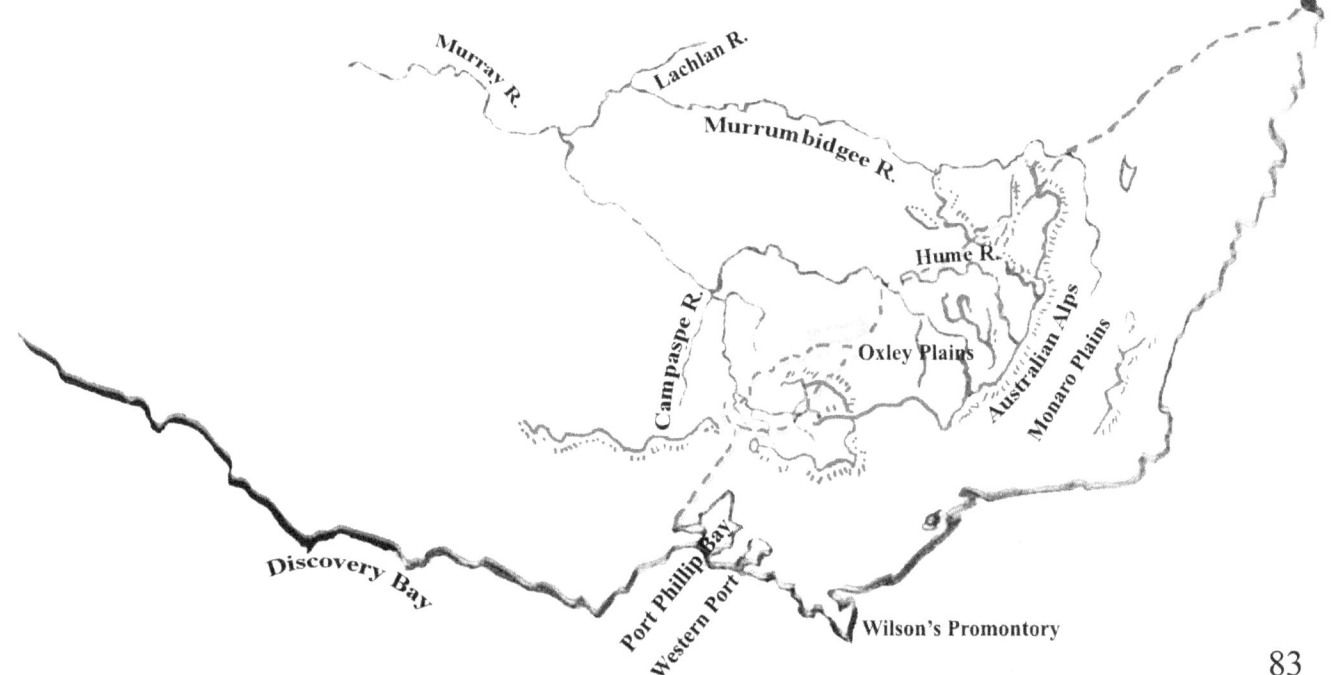

The great riddle of the rivers was to be answered by Captain Charles Sturt, who led two expeditions in his search for a solution. It is surely fitting that the great Australian-born explorer, Hamilton Hume, was with Sturt on the first of these expeditions.

It was 1828 when Sturt set out to follow in Oxley's steps along the Macquarie. Now you might think this was very unwise, as the thick, high reeds which had forced Oxley from its banks would surely do the same to Sturt. It was quite a different story for Sturt, however. You see, there had been a dreadful period of drought in the colony, and many streams that once flowed strongly were now trickling along. In some cases, indeed, they had dried up altogether, in the drought-ridden land of the west.

Sturt had to press on through dry, parched country. The heat was intense, often reaching 43 degrees. Later Sturt wrote about the horror of the drought. "The emus," he wrote, "with outstretched necks, gasping for breath, searched for water in vain and the native dog, so thin that he could hardly walk, seemed to implore some merciful hand to dispatch him."

At long last the explorers came to the banks of a stream flowing between banks at least 65 metres apart. Pelicans and other wild fowl were to be seen on its waters, and we can imagine just how excited the thirsty men were as they scrambled down the bank to the water. "Here at last," they thought, "there is plenty to drink." They were soon to be bitterly disappointed. The very first man to scoop up a handful, and hold it to his mouth, immediately spat it out in disgust.

"Salt!" he shouted, slapping the water in despair. It's as salty as the ocean!"

The man was making no mistake, for salt springs in the bed of the river made the water at this particular spot quite undrinkable. Fortunately, Hume was able to find a small pond of fresh water nearby, and both men and animals were able to drink their fill.

After naming the new river the *Darling* after Governor Darling, Sturt returned some distance along the Macquarie and then struck out for the

Castlereagh. He was able to follow its dry bed until it, too, reached the Darling. Sturt now knew where the Macquarie and the Castlereagh had their mouths. They flowed into the Darling. But where did the Darling flow? And what about all the other westward-flowing rivers? Where did they finally end?

The very next year, 1829, Sturt again set out to try finally to solve the riddle of the rivers. His plan was to follow the course of the Murrumbidgee River, hoping it would lead him eventually to the sea. When the group of men reached the banks of the Murrumbidgee, Sturt ordered that the boat they had carried overland in pieces be assembled and that a tree be felled and shaped into a small boat, or skiff. Then, leaving some of the men to make camp on the banks of the river, he took a small, picked band with him.

They had travelled for only a couple of days when Fate struck them a serious blow. The little skiff, which was being towed behind the whale-boat, struck a snag and sank. It had all the food on board. The men quickly raised the skiff to the surface again, but it was too late for water had already soaked into the salt meat and much of the food was spoiled. This unfortunate occurrence meant that the men were to be placed on short rations for the rest of the trip.

Before many more kilometres were travelled, the explorers were given their first piece of encouragement. They came to the junction of the Murrumbidgee and the Lachlan. Now, at last, men knew what happened to the Lachlan that had puzzled Oxley so many years before when it had hidden itself in swamps.

After the junction of the Lachlan and the Murrumbidgee had been passed, the men continued down the Murrumbidgee. One day they felt their boat begin to gather speed. The banks of the river seemed to become narrower and the water began to flow faster and faster. Suddenly they found their boat being "shot out", as Sturt tells us, "into a broad and noble river". They had reached the river which Hume had named after his father. It is a great pity that Sturt, who must have

guessed the river probably was the "Hume", decided to re-name it the *Murray* (after an influential English politician).

Sturt now felt that he knew the answer to the riddle of the rivers. He was certain that the Darling would soon meet with the Murray and that the Murray would then flow into the sea. We know that Sturt was right, but he was to have at least one very anxious moment before he could continue to try to prove this.

The explorers were floating along happily down the Murray when they suddenly saw a group of excited natives on a sandy spit. They were performing a fierce sort of dance, and it was obvious to the explorers that they would be very lucky to escape alive. Even though the explorers had guns, there were about 600 Aborigines in the group and there would have been little hope for the men in the boat. Hoping to frighten the others away, Sturt raised his gun and took careful aim at the closest Aborigines.

"At that very moment," Sturt later wrote, "when my hand was on the trigger and my eye was along the barrel, I was stopped by George Macleay, my second in command." Macleay had stopped Sturt from firing, because he had seen another group of natives rushing along the bank opposite to those on the sand-spit. It was a group of Aborigines to whom the explorers had given help only a couple of days before. One of the group was a giant warrior. Springing into the water, this giant struck out strongly towards the warlike group and, upon reaching them, he took their leader by the throat and pushed him back. Shaking his fist at the rest of the group, he warned them to leave the white strangers alone. It seems that he was a very important Aboriginal leader in the land, for Sturt and his men were allowed to pass without any further incident. Today we would say the explorers had experienced a very close call that day. They certainly knew their lives had indeed been spared.

Some days after their adventure with the Aborigines, the explorers arrived at the junction of the Murray and yet another large river. Sturt was certain that this new river, flowing in from their right, was the same Darling River that he had discovered the year before. To make certain of this, Sturt turned into the new river and began tracing it upstream. His party had travelled only a short distance when native fishing-traps across the river blocked their way. Wisely, Sturt decided not to disturb the traps and made his way back towards the Murray. In his own mind he was certain that the stream he had been following was the Darling. Of course we know today that he was right.

Continuing down the Murray, Sturt and his men eventually came to a large lake, which he called *Lake Alexandrina*. As Sturt had expected the Murray to end in the sea he was rather surprised to find it emptying its waters into this huge lake. He therefore explored the lake and, a couple of days later, found that the lake itself had an outlet into the Southern Ocean at Encounter Bay.

At last the riddle of the rivers seemed to have been solved. Sturt believed he had proved that the western rivers emptied their waters into the Darling or the Murray; that the Darling joined the Murray which then flowed on until it emptied its waters into the Southern Ocean. Nothing remained for Sturt to do now except to return home.

The journey homeward was to prove a tremendous task for Sturt and his men. They had now to row upstream against the current. Already tired and weak, they each had to take turns at the oars. For fifty-six weary days they struggled on, rowing under a fierce, merciless sun. Their food supply was low, and the men were so exhausted that they often fell asleep at the oars before they reached the junction with the Murrumbidgee. Then they had to struggle overland back to Sydney. At last the long journey was over, but it had been such a terrible experience that one of the men had lost his mind while Sturt himself had become temporarily blind.

The most baffling problem concerning the inland of Australia now appeared to have been solved. People now considered they knew what happened to the westward-flowing rivers of New South Wales. Of course there were many other explorers who helped to answer problems about our sunburnt country. There is not space in this little book to tell the full story of each of them, but some of the more important names should be mentioned. The Alps and Gippsland were explored by Paul Strzelecki. The northern area was explored by Leichhardt in 1844-6, by Kennedy in 1847 and 1848, by A. C. Gregory in 1855-6 and in 1858, and by Burke and Wills in 1860-1.

It was in the years 1859-62 that the continent was first successfully and completely crossed from south to north. The route of this journey made by John McDouall Stuart was soon to be followed by the Overland Telegraph Line.

Edward John Eyre was able to link the eastern and western states by his journey around the shores of the Great Australian Bight in 1839-41. In later years the Forrest brothers also explored the Nullarbor Plain carefully, and later John Forrest explored much of the south-western area of the state of Western Australia.

In the early 1870s separate expeditions were made by Warburton, Giles and Gosse into the central and western areas of Australia's vast inland. It was while making his expedition that Gosse found a strange hill. "It was one immense rock rising abruptly from the plain," Gosse said. He discovered caves in the rock and these were filled with

excellent examples of aboriginal drawings. Strange, vivid colours seemed to match and mingle on the slopes of the giant monolith, and so steep were the sides that Gosse reported that it would be almost impossible to climb up them. Gosse was right. Except for one place on the side of the rock it is almost impossible to climb. This huge, red monolith has become a famous tourist attraction. It was given the name Ayer's Rock but is now known by its Aboriginal name — *Uluru*. It is regarded by the local Aboriginal people as a sacred site and they would prefer it if tourists showed respect for this fact by not climbing it.

By the time the explorers we have mentioned had completed their work, most of the inland areas of Australia had been visited. Settlers with their sheep and cattle soon followed the inland explorers, wherever good pasture had been found. Around the long coastline of Australia other important settlements had in the meantime been established.

While all the explorers mentioned deserve the credit they are given, it should also be remembered that, from the very beginning, Aborigines played a significant role in the exploration of this continent. In 1791 an expedition led by Governor Phillip included two Eora men, Colbee and Boladeree, from the Sydney region. Paul Strzlecki and James Macarthur, who explored the Alps and Gippsland would probably have died of starvation if it had not been for the hunting skills of Charlie Tara, an Aboriginal guide. Such was also the case when the guides Carley and Harry used their skills to find food to keep the Leichhardt party alive. Space does not allow for the stories of the wonderful loyalty of Wylie (who accompanied Eyre) and of Jackey-Jackey (who miraculously survived to tell the tragic story of the Kennedy expedition). It was an Aboriginal tribe who cared for John King , the sole survivor of the Burke and Wills expedition until a search party located him and, as we have seen, it was the incredible action of a giant Aboriginal leader that saved the members of the Sturt party from almost certain death.

Chapter Eight

New Colonies in Australia

IT was as early as 1803 that a party of 300 convicts, with fifty marines to guard them, arrived at Port Phillip. They were under the command of Colonel David Collins. They did not stay long, because Collins considered the soil too sandy and was unable to find a suitable stream of fresh water. He decided to cross Bass Strait and make a new settlement on the banks of the Derwent River. Collins chose a spot beneath the towering height of Mount Wellington, and thus the settlement of Hobart was begun.

Another settlement was made in *northern* Van Diemen's Land, in 1804 on the lovely verdant banks of the Tamar River. The site was twice changed before, in 1806, the settlers were moved to the spot that is now occupied by the beautiful city of Launceston.

Van Diemen's Land was declared to be a separate colony in 1825. It was in 1855 that the people of the island decided to change the name to *Tasmania*, in honour of its Dutch discoverer.

For more than fifty years convicts were transported to Van Diemen's Land and on the bank of an inlet about 100 kilometres from Hobart the cruel prison known as Port Arthur was built and, although the last convicts arrived in 1853, it was in use from 1830 until 1877. Today visitors are able to visit the ruins of the prison settlement and get some idea of the cruel treatment suffered by those early prisoners. Tourists are also able to visit, with respect, the memorial to more than thirty men, women and children who were massacred there by a demented gunman in late April, 1996. Shocked by this appalling act John Howard (Prime Minister, 1996 - 2007) introduced a scheme to buy back a great number of dangerous firearms and ensured laws were passed to restrict future gun sales.

After the explorations of Hume and Hovell, people became more interested in the southern section of the mainland. Certain farmers decided to bring their flocks and herds to the area. In 1834 the Henty family packed up their belongings and sailed from Launceston. They chose a spot on Portland Bay as the site for their new home. They found the land to be rich and productive. Others, learning of the good fortune of the Hentys, followed them across.

Pioneer settlers were also soon to re-explore the Port Phillip district. A party led by John Batman found, in 1835, that there was certainly much good land in the area. Highly delighted, Batman decided to settle there. He then did something that had never before been done in Australia. He drew up a "treaty" or agreement with the natives. In return for knives, blankets, tomahawks, scissors, looking-glasses, handkerchiefs and other goods, Batman was to receive from the natives about 225,000 hectares of land. Batman signed the treaty and eight natives "made their marks" upon it, and the Tasmanians then went off to pack their belongings and make preparations for settlement at Port Phillip. Whether or not the eight Aborigines understood what they were agreeing to is certainly open to question.

Almost at the same time as Batman's party began to make their settlement, another party led by John Pascoe Fawkner appeared on the scene and they liked the banks of the Yarra so much that they insisted upon settling in the same area as Batman.

The spot chosen by Batman as the "site for a village" was a particularly splendid area about nine kilometers from the mouth of the Yarra. So quickly did the Port Phillip district develop that, in 1836, Governor Bourke decided to send Captain Lonsdale and a group of soldiers and police to make sure law and order were maintained. In 1837 Bourke named the growing settlement "Melbourne" in honour of the British Prime Minister. The next year John Pascoe Fawkner, who had already opened a store and a hotel, started a newspaper, the *Melbourne Advertiser* and by 1851 the southern settlement had grown so quickly that it was separated from New South Wales and became the colony of Victoria.

It was not until 1826 that any attempt was made to settle the south-western shores of Australia but on Christmas Day of that year a military garrison and a group of convicts arrived to establish a tiny settlement at King George Sound. Captain James Stirling explored the Swan River area and was convinced Great Britain should encourage free settlers to come. The government agreed, on the condition that the settlers met all the costs.

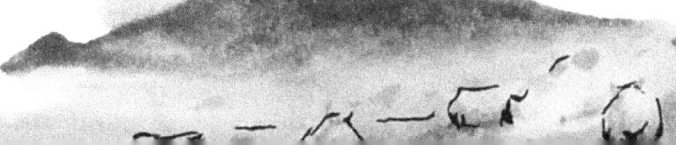

On May 2nd, 1829 Captain Charles Howe Fremantle arrived and took possession of the land in the name of the King and on June 1st the first settlers were put ashore on a beach near the mouth of the Swan River. There they huddled together with their belongings — their stores, tables, chairs, beds and even a piano — in wind and driving rain. It was not a very promising way for a settlement to begin!

Stirling arrived about three weeks later and built a fort (Fremantle) at the mouth of the Swan River and then moved further upstream to a river basin which he decided would be the site for the settlement of *Perth*. Settlers were not "granted" land but could purchase it. After the best land was bought other settlers established a number of small settlements along the coast between Perth and Cape Leeuwin.

For some years the settlers who purchased the land found it very difficult to find labourers to work it or to help with the construction of public buildings and roads. To overcome this problem the people of Western Australia, at a time when transportation of convicts was being stopped in other colonies, actually asked Britain for a supply of convict labour. From 1852 until 1868 ten thousand male convicts were transported to Western Australia.

In time the discovery of gold at Coolgardie in 1892 by A.W. Bayley and W. Ford and at Kalgoorlie by Patrick ("Paddy") Hannon in 1889 led to the opening of fabulously rich goldfields.

Good fortune has continued to smile upon Western Australia. In 1952, a grazier named Lang Hancock became lost under thick cloud while flying his light aircraft. He flew below the cloud line and into a gorge in the Hamersley Ranges. He noticed the gorge had rust-coloured walls and believed they were oxidized iron. Later he returned and collected samples of iron ore chips from the spot and was delighted to discover they were of very high quality. His discovery has led to a tremendous expansion of mining in the Pilbara Region.

The Hamersley mine at Mount Tom Price was opened in 1962 and within five years another four mines were established and have brought tremendous wealth to Western Australia and to the nation.

Another early settlement was made on the east coast of Saint Vincent's Gulf, in South Australia, as a result of twelve letters appearing in the *Morning Chronicle*, a London newspaper. Each letter claimed to be *A Letter from Sydney, the Principal Town of Australia*. The author was Edward Gibbon Wakefield, who had never been to Sydney and was actually spending three years in prison for trying to elope with a young heiress! However, the two major ideas expressed in the letters impressed a number of influential people. Wakefield's suggestions were that:

a. land should not be granted but should be sold at a "sufficient price" so that only rich people could afford to buy it; and
b. other people should be encouraged to come as labourers who would work hard and save their money so that, in time, they would be able to buy land.

Soon people who were interested in establishing a settlement based on Wakefield's ideas formed the *South Australian Society* and made their way to Kangaroo Island where they waited while Colonel William Light went to Saint Vincent's Gulf to select the site for settlement.

On 21st November, 1836, Light selected the delightful spot on the Torrens River where the lovely city of Adelaide was eventually built and the rest of the group soon arrived to begin the settlement. Once "overlanders" began to arrive with their cattle, and 537 German Lutherans came in 1839 seeking a safe place to practise their religious beliefs, the new colony became firmly established.

By the end of the 1840s there were many separate settlements around the coastline of Australia and settlers were beginning to fill the empty spaces, wherever a good water supply and fertile land made this possible.

Chapter Nine

Days of Gold

SO far, of course, our sunburnt country had grown slowly and steadily. However, the people of the different settlements tended to think of themselves as Tasmanians or Western Australians or New South Welshmen. It was at this time that something dramatic was to happen that would help Australia to develop at a tremendous pace and, at the same time, help men and women to begin thinking of themselves as *Australians*.

What magic could possibly bring about the amazing change from slow to fast growth? What magician could be at work causing settlements to spring up almost overnight in areas where no other whites had lived before? What spell caused shipload after shipload of immigrants to begin flocking to our shores? What fever was it that possessed men and women, making them leave their homes and their jobs to go inland and live in a tent?

The fever, the magic, the magician and the spell were all one — GOLD! The news that gold had been discovered in New South Wales in 1851 spread like wildfire throughout the world and a new life, a faster, more thrilling life, came to the land.

Perhaps you will be surprised to find that gold had actually been found long before 1851 in Australia. There were, in fact, several finds earlier than this date, but not many people knew anything about them and the early Governors were keen to keep them secret in case a gold rush occurred, making it impossible to keep control of the convicts. James McBrien, a surveyor, found gold near the Fish River in 1823. A convict picked up some too, but he was thought to have stolen it, so he was flogged. Then other people began to find it. Two geologists, one an explorer, Count Strzelecki, and the other, a clergyman, W. B. Clarke, made finds in the Blue Mountains and to the west between 1839 and 1842, while shepherds and graziers picked up specimens around Bathurst and Wellington.

One particularly interesting find was a piece of gold found at *Yorkey's Corner* and *Lewis Ponds Creek*, near *Guyong*. The shepherd who found it had handed it to William Tipple Smith and he in turn had handed it to a government official, Deas Thomson. Another interesting detail was that in 1850 Smith wrote a little guide to gold-finders in which he mentioned Lewis Ponds Creek and Yorkey's Corner.

Gold discoveries in California, USA, were causing great numbers of people to throng to the United States. So many people were leaving New South Wales in the hope of "striking it rich" in America that the Government began to hope a rich find could be made here in order to tempt the settlers to come back. No more convicts were being sent to New South Wales after 1840 and so the guarding and supervision of convicts was no longer a problem. However, losing great numbers to California caused a host of other problems and the government needed to do something to stop the loss. Therefore it was decided to offer a reward of ten thousand pounds (about $25,000) to anyone who could discover a goldfield. This was a great deal of money in 1850.

One of the "fortyniners" to go to California was Edward Hammond Hargraves. Before going to California, the 115 kilograms Hargraves had been a sailor, an overseer, a farmer, a publican, a shipping agent and a grazier. He was surprised to find the gold-bearing country in California was very similar to certain areas in New South Wales.

"I tell you, my friend," he confided to another of the diggers, "the resemblance of this country to that in New South Wales is amazing, especially to one area I know near the town of Bathurst."

"That might be true," answered the other, "but surely it doesn't mean there is gold in the hills near Bathurst."

"Perhaps not," agreed Hargraves," but it seems to me that the rock in the two places is so much alike there *could* be gold in the hills of home. Anyway, I haven't had much luck here. Most of the good places have been pegged out by other diggers. I'm off home to New South Wales to test out my theory."

There is no proof of this, of course, but one is left wondering if Hargraves had also managed to get a copy of William Tipple Smith's booklet because, once he had arrived in Sydney, Hargraves called at the inn at Guyong. *Down the creek which flowed past the inn was a spot called Yorkey's Corner.* Two local guides at the inn knew the Summer Hill Creek area well and Hargraves asked them to help him explore the creek in his search for gold. These two men, John Lister and James Tom, led Hargraves to the spot known as *Lewis Ponds*. Hargraves trembled with excitement for all around him were hills, valleys and rocks just like the ones he had seen in California. Now he felt certain of success, especially if he had, in fact, read Smith's booklet.

Taking his pan from the saddle-bag on his horse, Hargraves stooped towards the water. He filled the pan with sand, mud, silt and water from the bed of the Ponds and then began to swish the pan steadily back and forth, letting the water and lighter particles of silt slosh over the edge. At last there were only a few heavy grains in the bottom of the pan, and these grains had a rich, soft gleam about them. Hargraves gave a shout of joy, for these heavy grains were specks of gold!

Eagerly Hargraves washed another pan of earth, and another and another. He was laughing and shouting with happiness, for out of the five pans of earth he washed that day he found gold in four.

When he had recovered a little from the first exciting moments of discovery, Hargraves turned to Lister and said, "This is a memorable day in the history of New South Wales. I shall be a baronet, you will be knighted, my old horse will be stuffed, put in a glass case and sent to the British Museum." Now most of this prophecy did not come true, but no one can deny that the day on which gold was found at Lewis Ponds was indeed a "memorable" one in our history. Hargraves hurried into Bathurst to spread the news of the gold to be found and before long there were 1,000 diggers in the area, with some of them "striking it rich". Hargraves, of course, was given the ten thousand pounds reward.

In the Bible we read of a place called Ophir, and it is said that King Solomon had a great fortune of gold from this place. Because people hoped to find great fortunes at the goldfield discovered by Hargraves, it, too, was called Ophir, and to the diggings flocked men and women of all descriptions, from all walks of life and from many countries. Some rode in drays or on horseback; others carried swags on their backs; some wheeled their few belongings in wheelbarrows and trudged the weary kilometres from Sydney. I suppose they were thankful for the road Governor Macquarie had ordered Cox to build over the mountains.

Soon there were thousands at the diggings and hosts of tents and huts were appearing everywhere. Henry Lawson's poem "'The Roaring Days" well describes the exciting scene.

The yellow mounds of mullock
   With spots of red and white,
The scattered quartz that glistened
   Like diamonds in light;
The azure line of ridges,
   The bush of darkest green,
The little homes of calico
   That dotted all the scene.

There is no doubt that Hargraves's find brought fame, fortune and people to New South Wales, but at the same time it caused a great deal of concern in other parts of Australia. Colonies that were already very small suddenly found they were in danger of losing most of their able-bodied men, because these men were all rushing away to New South Wales. In particular the Government and wealthy businessmen of Victoria were greatly worried.

Victoria had been separated from New South Wales only a few months before Hargraves's discovery. The leaders of the new State were very anxious to prove that Victoria could succeed on her own, and now it seemed that this might not be so because there would be too few people left for the State to carry on. In desperation the authorities in Victoria offered a reward to anyone who could find gold within 320 kilometres of Melbourne.

The Government of Victoria was soon to feel very thankful that they had made this offer. The thrilling news became known that vastly rich fields had been found at Ballarat and at Bendigo. A third field was also discovered at Clunes. It seemed that the problems in Victoria were over.

People now began to pour into Victoria. These new fields were even richer than those in New South Wales, and diggers flocked across the border. Others came in ships from Europe and America. Chinese also began to arrive in great numbers, many of them having to disembark at Robe, a little settlement on the coast of South Australia. This was done so that the ships' owners could avoid paying a tax at Port Phillip for each of the Chinese miners. From Robe the Chinese miners had to carry their belongings hundreds of kilometres to the diggings. On the way some of them stopped to wash their clothes and to gather water at a little stream and discovered gold in the stream at Ararat.

The largest ships available were put on the England-Australia run, and each ship was crammed full of hopeful diggers when it sailed into Port Phillip. Often the ships could not easily sail out again because the "gold fever" would strike the sailors and, deserting their ships, they too would make their way to the diggings. These, indeed, were exciting days!

The young Government of Victoria was now faced with new problems. Where there had previously been too few people, there were now too many. Thousands of extra mouths had to be fed. Food and drink for these mouths had quickly to be found and taken to the goldfields. Roads had to be built, so that this could be done more efficiently. It was also necessary to employ and pay extra policemen to enforce law and order on the diggings. As money had to be found to pay for these tasks, it was decided to make all diggers pay a fee, called a "licence fee". In return for this fee, each digger was to receive a licence allowing him to dig on the goldfields.

Now, at first, the people did not seem to worry very much about the fee but, as the gold became harder to find and shafts had to be dug deeper and deeper, the diggers became more and more discontented and dissatisfied with their lot. They claimed that the Government should build better roads so that goods could be brought more easily from Melbourne, thus keeping the prices of these goods low enough for the miners to pay. They argued, too, that all the diggers should have a right to vote, so that they would have the chance to elect men who would represent them properly in Parliament. They also demanded that Members of Parliament should be paid so that any man, whether rich or poor, could sit in Parliament. Most of all, the diggers hated the system of licences. It was not hard for a lucky man, who had found gold, to pay the fee, but it was a lot of money for the unlucky digger to have to pay. Many of them finally refused to do so.

In order to catch the diggers who were not paying their fees, the police paid visits to the goldfields and carried out "licence inspections". As soon as the policemen appeared, those men whose licences were not up to date would scamper off into the bush to hide, or would go far underground into disused shafts and tunnels, for they knew that if they were caught they would be chained to a tree for half a day. There they would have to stand, under the scorching sun and without water, until the police came back to release them.

Not many miners were caught, however, as the shout "Joey, Joey" went up the moment any policeman was seen in the distance. This was the signal for all those without licences to scatter and hide.

There was often trouble and bad feeling between the law and the diggers, and finally this bad feeling came to an armed conflict at Ballarat in 1854. Three miners had been arrested and jailed for burning down a hotel. The hotelkeeper, according to the miners, had murdered one of the diggers, and some of the other men had angrily burnt his hotel to the ground. When three of the diggers were arrested and jailed, the other miners sent a deputation to the Governor, asking that the three men be released and that the other demands of the miners, regarding licence fees and votes, be met. However, the three men were kept in jail, and the Governor refused to grant the other claims of the diggers.

The angry diggers decided that they would organize a revolt. They made a bonfire of their licences, ran a blue flag with a silver Southern Cross in its centre to the top of a pole, built a stockade and elected a big Irishman, named Peter Lalor, as their "Commander-in-Chief".

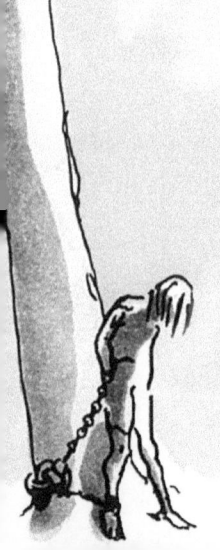

Standing on a tree-stump, with the muzzle of his rifle in his left hand and the butt-end resting on his foot, Lalor called loudly to the men gathered around him, "It is my duty, now, to swear you in, and to take with you the oath to be faithful to the Southern Cross. Hear me with attention. The man who, after this solemn oath, does not stand by our standard, is a coward at heart. I order all men who do not intend to take the oath, to leave the meeting at once." No-one made a move to leave, so Lalor gave the men the order to fall in and then, after him, they repeated this oath:

"We swear by the Southern Cross to stand truly by each other, and fight to defend our rights and liberties."

And they *did* stand truly by each other, for when the troopers attacked their stockade the fight was fierce and bloody. The diggers, however, were not well trained and they were very poorly armed. The fiery little revolt was soon over, and more than twenty diggers were either dead or dying. Lalor had been wounded, but friends had hidden him so that he would not be killed. Five soldiers were also either dead or dying. A hundred of the diggers were taken prisoner and the rebellion at the EUREKA STOCKADE was over.

Although the actual revolt at Eureka ended in failure, it did show how strongly the diggers felt about their claims. Governor Hotham ordered an inquiry into the rebellion and into the demands made by the diggers. As a result of this inquiry the hated licence fees were discontinued. Instead a "duty" or fee had to be paid to the Government on all gold leaving the country. This meant that only the lucky diggers were being asked to pay anything.

The story of the Eureka Stockade is re-enacted regularly at night, in an exciting "sound-and-light show" on Sovereign Hill in Ballarat. Many tourists flock to see it, including coachloads of excited schoolchildren.

Miners had fought for the things they considered to be right, and the ideas and ideals of these men were to live on. Their pioneer spirit of freedom and fair dealing for all was to continue to be important long after the rushes to Ballarat and Bendigo and to the other fields of Kalgoorlie and Coolgardie (discovered later in Western Australia) were over. These men had shown that they were prepared to fight and even to die for their belief in the freedom and equal standing of all people. They wanted a vote for everyone, whether rich or poor. They believed in payment of elected Members of Parliament, so that any person could afford to become a member, and they believed in frequent elections. These men, and others like them, were to continue struggling for these ideals until they were all finally won.

There were many results of the gold discoveries in Australia. Some of these were:– there was an amazing increase in population, the number of people in Australia growing from 405,000 in 1850 to 1,168,000 in 1861; towns and villages sprang up where there had been only land before; roads and wharves were built to serve these new towns; a wonderful new industry was helping to make Australia rich, and more than £142 million (about $300 million) worth of gold was won in the thirty years after 1850. Determined, thinking men like those at Eureka were to help cause remarkable changes in the politics and government of Australia within the next few years.

There were two other results of the gold discoveries that should be mentioned. The first was that bushranging once again became a menace to decent people, and the second was that a very famous coaching service had its beginnings in the days of the gold discoveries.

Many were the occasions that coaches, travelling along the rough bush tracks, would suddenly come to a spot where a fallen tree, lying across the road, would block the way. When any coach was forced to stop in this way it meant that the driver and passengers needed to keep a sharp look-out, for it was more than likely that one, two, or several men would come swiftly riding out from cover, masks over their faces and guns pointing straight in front of them. Those travelling in the coach would then be informed, "This is a stick-up", and they would be robbed of their money, gold or jewellery.

Some of the stories of men like Thunderbolt, Moonlight, and the Ned Kelly Gang would make your blood run cold. Often the stories told about these bushrangers would make them out to be men of great skill and courage. People should not forget that the bushrangers frightened and robbed and sometimes even killed those who happened to pass their way. Decent people were able to travel more easily and comfortably when the last ruffians were finally hunted down.

When Freeman Cobb came to Australia from America, he hoped to make his fortune by digging for gold. He was not a lucky digger, and so he decided to try to make his fortune another way. He could see that the diggers and others in Victoria needed a good, fast, comfortable means of travel. With three friends he therefore went into business, beginning the famous firm of Cobb and Co. So that the best coaches available could be used by the firm, Cobb sent to America for them.

Nothing was too good for Cobb and Co. For years it was a thrill for the people to see the well-painted, clean looking coaches, drawn by beautifully groomed horses, setting out on their run.

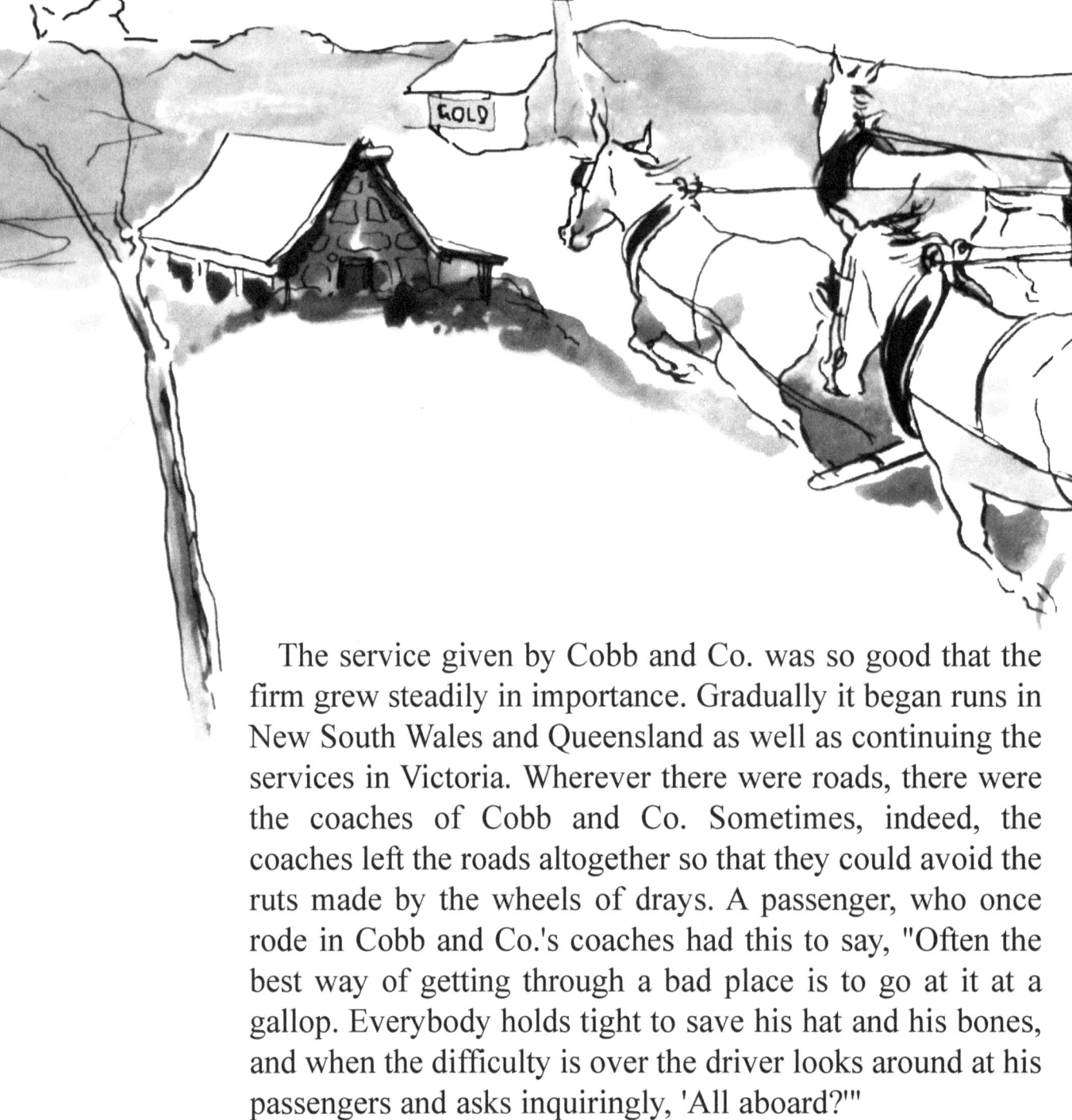

The service given by Cobb and Co. was so good that the firm grew steadily in importance. Gradually it began runs in New South Wales and Queensland as well as continuing the services in Victoria. Wherever there were roads, there were the coaches of Cobb and Co. Sometimes, indeed, the coaches left the roads altogether so that they could avoid the ruts made by the wheels of drays. A passenger, who once rode in Cobb and Co.'s coaches had this to say, "Often the best way of getting through a bad place is to go at it at a gallop. Everybody holds tight to save his hat and his bones, and when the difficulty is over the driver looks around at his passengers and asks inquiringly, 'All aboard?'"

It seems that a coach-ride in those days was quite an adventure. However, the teams of horses and the big coaches must have made a grand sight in the early morning's mist. With blue saddle-cloths on the horses, silver trimming on the finest of the harnesses, the driver wearing an air of importance and the company's flag fluttering in the breeze, the coaches of Cobb and Co. were splendid indeed.

Chapter Ten

Men of Industry

THE discovery of gold brought wonderful changes to our country. It must not be thought, however, that the gold industry was the only one helping Australia's development during the second half of the nineteenth century. There were many others, and men connected with some of those industries were to become world leaders in the discovery of new techniques and the invention of new machines.

Men like Macarthur and Marsden had pioneered the sheep industry in New South Wales. There were many others to follow these two, and both the sheep and cattle industries quickly developed. Squatters with their flocks and herds soon spread into the areas of good pasture discovered by the explorers, and Australia was shortly producing all the meat, wool, hides and tallow for her own needs with enough left over to begin exporting these products.

Overseas, the products of our sheep and cattle industries were found to equal the best in the world. But the people in England began to grow tired of the salted meat being sent from Australia, and said that they wanted *fresh* meat from our country. Now this was very difficult, because in those days there were no ships with refrigeration chambers. Hundreds tried to solve the problem. The man who finally succeeded was Thomas Sutcliffe Mort.

Mort had already made his name in the world of industry. He was the first man to conduct regular wool sales in Sydney, and soon wool-buyers from all over the world began to arrive in Sydney for the sales. The wool sales were exciting to watch. Everyone seemed to be calling out at once, each man shouting his bid in the hope that he would obtain some of Australia's world-famous wool.

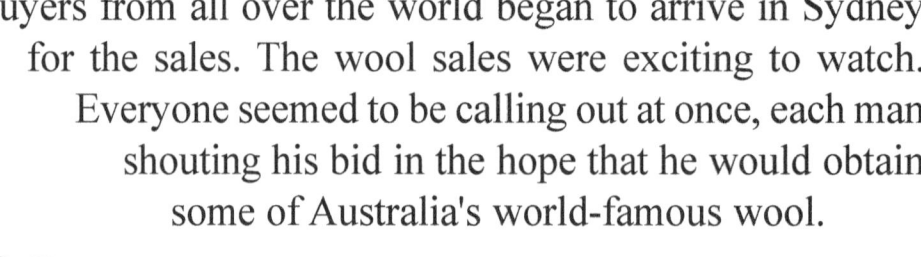

106

To listen to these excited buyers from places as far apart as Great Britain and Japan, one would wonder how the auctioneer could possibly decide the highest bidder; but he could, and finally the particular wool being sold was "knocked down" to the happy buyer.

People in Sydney are able to visit a dock in Woolwich which was established by Mort. The first steamer built at Mort's Dock slipped down into the water in 1856.

A man of energy, Mort was a director of the first railway company in New South Wales. He owned a splendid dairy farm at Bodalla, and it was here that his wife had a lovely little stone church built in his memory. He also took an active interest in the copper, silver and coal mining industries.

Although he was a very busy man, Mort was ready to give his support to any new, worth-while venture and decided to try to find a way of sending fresh meat to England. In 1866 he met an engineer named Nicolle, who had been experimenting with refrigeration. "I'll supply the money," Mort told Nicolle, "if you can only find some way of keeping meat fresh for long periods."

For years experiments were carried out. So many times did the men meet with failure that Mort said, "Not once but ten thousand times I wished that we had never been born." Yet, in spite of their disappointments and setbacks, the experimenters continued, for they knew how important to Australia was their success. At last they were able to build a freezing-works in which meat could be kept fresh.

The next step was to refrigerate a ship, so that frozen meat could be sent to England. Unfortunately, the first trial shipment was a failure. Pipes carrying the ammonia used in the freezing process were strained by movements of the ship and began to leak. The meat had to be unloaded and the ship sailed without it. Mort was terribly upset. He had already spent £100,000 (about $225,000) on the project, and now it seemed that all his efforts had been in vain.

The year 1879 was to tell a different story. Another attempt was made, and the *Strathleven* reached London with a cargo of frozen meat and butter. All the food was in perfect condition. This was indeed a triumph for Australia. Unhappily, however, the man who had made it all possible did not live to see the victory. Thomas Sutcliffe Mort had died a year earlier.

Another industry to grow quickly with the spread of settlement was the wheat industry. Several men were to play important roles in its development. One of these was Robert Smith, who invented a "stump-jump" plough, so that land could be cultivated even though some of the tree-stumps had not been removed. This wonderful plough made it possible to use land which otherwise would have been difficult or impossible to cultivate.

Once the wheat was ready for harvest, the stripper invented by John Ridley, and later Hugh McKay's harvester, helped the farmer to bring in his crop much more speedily. Indeed, so good was McKay's Sunshine Harvester that he soon had orders for it from many parts of Australia and the world.

Diseases known as rust or smut caused one of the serious problems of the wheat industry. In the early days farmers sometimes lost their entire crops as a result of these diseases. It was very important, therefore, to find some way of defeating them.

In 1886 William Farrer began to experiment with wheat. He decided that, to defeat rust and smut it was necessary to develop a type of wheat

that could resist them. From other countries he imported many varieties of wheat. He grew them in rows, labelling each row. When the wheat was in flower, he crossed the pollen from one variety with another. Gradually he developed several types of wheat that would each suit special conditions in Australia. Some varieties would ripen very early, while others he developed could be sown in the drier western areas where the rainfall was less than 38 centimetres a year. It was in 1902 that Farrer developed a strong drought-resistant grain which was called "Federation". Do you know why it was given this name? If you do not know, I think you will work out the answer after you have read the next chapter of *Our Sunburnt Country*.

Along the coastal strip of northern New South Wales and into Queensland another important crop was now being grown commercially. This was sugar cane. The first man successfully to grow sugar cane in Australia was Thomas Alison Scott. In 1817 he brought sugar canes from Tahiti and grew them in the Sydney Gardens. He also grew canes at the convict settlement at Port Macquarie in 1827 and gradually small areas were grown along the Tweed, Richmond and Clarence Rivers and into the south-eastern corner of Queensland. Then, in 1863 Louis Hope not only established a plantation on 20 acres (8 hectares) in the Moreton Bay district but he built a small mill so that he could grow, cut and crush his own cane and sell the sugar himself. Hope is known as "the father of the Australian sugar industry" and he deserves this title, for he was the industry's commercial pioneer. It is unfortunate that Hope began a practice that was to leave a blot on our history. In 1864 he had native workers from the South Sea Islands brought by boat to Moreton Bay. These men would work for very little money and other sugar-growers also began to employ them. Sometimes the men came willingly, but there were occasions when they were "black-birded". That is, they were carried off from their homes by force.

Many people felt that the "Kanakas", or South Sea Islanders, were being treated little better than slaves, and it was a good thing that the Government decided in 1906 to send them back to their homes.

Even though dark-skinned South Sea Islanders could no longer be employed, the sugar industry continued to grow. Today, more than a hundred-and-forty years after Louis Hope planted his first crop, the industry which he founded is a most important one on the tropical north-eastern coast of Australia. Some of the by-products of the sugar cane industry include ethanol, methylated spirits, mulch for gardens, Caneite, molasses, golden syrup, treacle and rum.

Other crops that have been important in Australia's development have included bananas and other tropical fruits, grapes and wine, other fruits and vegetables, rice, canola, timber and wood chips.

As well as important agricultural industries, others were developing in Australia by the beginning of the 20th Century. Iron had been made at the Fitzroy works, near Mittagong, and at the Eskbank works, near Lithgow. George and Charles Hoskins, who owned the Eskbank works, decided to join forces with the Australian Iron and Steel Company at Port Kembla.

The most important centres for the manufacture of iron and steel were Newcastle and Port Kembla. Long, brown, ore-carrying boats brought the iron ore to these two centres, for they are many kilometres from the deposits of iron ore. Most of the ore came from Yampi Sound in Western Australia and from the Iron Knob area in South Australia. Why is it, do you think, that the steelworks were not closer to the iron ore deposits? The answer is that there are very important coal-fields near Newcastle and Port Kembla, and even more coal than iron ore is needed in making steel.

Chapter Eleven

Birth of a Nation

IN the previous chapter you read about some of the most important industries developing in Australia by the end of the nineteenth century. There were many people who felt that Australia was a rich young country and that plans should be made for her defence, just in case some other nation should consider attacking this land. In the matter of defence, then, the people in the different colonies were beginning to think of themselves as *Australians* and not just as Queenslanders, or New South Welshmen, Victorians, Tasmanians, Western Australians, South Australians or members of any one particular colony or territory. These people felt that, as well as self-government for the colonies, there should be a *Federal* Government to make decisions about things that affected all Australians, and State Governments should concern themselves only with State matters.

One of the men who worked particularly hard for a united Australia was Sir Henry Parkes. He was a determined, forceful man and a great speaker. It was largely through his efforts that education in New South Wales had become free, compulsory and secular. Once Parkes, and others like him, began to speak, the people in the various States soon realized the importance of unity.

In one of his most famous addresses Parkes, still a powerful-looking man although becoming aged and stooped, declared, "The time has come for the creation on this Australian continent of an Australian Government with a Federal Parliament for the conduct of National business." As he spoke the people watching this fine-looking man with the flowing white beard could not help but feel that he was right.

Finally it was decided that there should be a Federal Government to take charge of defence, foreign affairs, postal services, taxation, immigration and other matters that would affect all people in Australia.

It was on 1st January, 1901, that the Australian Commonwealth was born. Lord Hopetoun was appointed Governor General and Edmund Barton became the first Prime Minister. Today the Commonwealth Parliament consists of an Upper House, known as the *Senate*, and a Lower House, called the *House of Representatives*. There is an election of all Members of the House of Representatives once every three years, and there is an election for *half* the total number of Senators every three years; thus each Senator sits for a total of six years, and there is never a completely new Upper House.

There are many political parties in Australia today, and each party has candidates trying to win seats whenever elections are held. The strongest parties are the Labor Party, the Liberal Party, and the National Party. The Liberal and National Parties have usually joined together to form a coalition.

Since 1927 Parliament has met at Canberra, the modern Federal Capital of Australia. This beautiful garden city was designed by Walter Burley Griffin of Chicago, and is one of the loveliest capital cities in the world. Magnificent buildings are surrounded by many varieties of trees, well-kept lawns and gardens of massed blooms. Beautiful avenues of blossoming trees delight visitors to Canberra in the springtime, while historic, picturesque buildings, such as "Yarralumla", contrast charmingly with the many others of modern design. "Yarralumla" is the home of the Governor General when he is in Canberra. It was once the homestead on a pastoral station. The Library, the Academy of Science, the Art Gallery, the High Court, the War Memorial, the National Gallery and Australia's magnificent Parliament House are all impressive buildings in the lovely city of Canberra.

After Federation in 1901, the most important job for the Federal Government was to build firm foundations upon which our nation could safely grow. One of the early Prime Ministers, Alfred Deakin, worked especially hard to achieve this. Deakin first became Prime Minister in 1903. He decided to protect Australia's young industries by placing an import duty on certain foreign goods. This meant that anyone importing goods into Australia had to pay a form of tax on them when they arrived.

Deakin also felt that the standard of living in Australia should be kept high. To ensure this, an Act called the Immigration Restriction Act (often referred to as the "*White Australia Policy*") was passed.

Although it was claimed that the most important reason for passing the Act was the fear that Australian workers might otherwise find it difficult to keep their jobs and earn a good living, the White Australia Policy was a deliberate and discriminatory attempt to keep Asian people and people with other than "white" skins out of the country. This policy required any intending immigrant to sit a dictation test. But the test did not have to be in the language of the applicant or, for that matter, in English! The test could be given in *any language*, including any language completely foreign to the applicant. There was no appeal.

This shameful Act was to last for many years.

Other Acts that brought shame to this first Parliament were the Act that disqualified Aboriginal natives of Australia from being able to vote in elections and, in 1908, an Act which stated that Aboriginal Australians were not eligible to receive an Invalid or an Old Age Pension. It was a long time before these insults to the Aboriginal people, whose ancestors had lived in this land for so many thousands of years, were corrected.

Indeed, it was not until 1959 that the "dictation test" was replaced with the entry permit system and it was not until 1967 that the Australian people in a referendum overwhelmingly (90%) voted for the franchise (the right to vote) to be extended to Aboriginal Australians.

As well as working to protect Australian industries and, although misguided, doing what they thought was best to protect Australian workers, members of our first National Parliament also took steps to make sure that Australia herself could be defended if attacked. Plans were made to build a strong army and navy, and orders were sent to England's shipyards for the construction of Australia's first warships, a battleship to be called the *Australia* and two cruisers to be known as the *Sydney* and the *Melbourne*.

It was a most fortunate thing that Deakin and the Parliament had begun to plan for a strong army and navy, for Australia was soon to find herself fighting as a nation for all those ideals held dear by her people.

Chapter Twelve

A Nation at War

AFTER Federation, the Commonwealth of Australia was indeed one nation, but a nation which did not really come of age until the terrible days of the First World War. When, in 1914, Britain found herself in danger, the members of her family rallied to her side. Australia offered whole-hearted support. Andrew Fisher, who became Prime Minister in the early part of the war, made this famous statement, "Australia will help and defend the mother-country to our last man and our last shilling."

On 4th August, 1914, Great Britain declared war on Germany and we, too, were at war.

An army had to be quickly organized and this task was given to General Bridges. Recruiting centres were hurriedly set up and young men came from everywhere to volunteer their services. Some travelled perhaps five hundred kilometres on horseback and then hundreds of kilometres farther by train for the honour of standing in a queue to join the army. Farmers left their homesteads, doctors their surgeries, teachers their schoolrooms and miners their tools. This army of men grew and grew. The Australian Imperial Force was born!

For many of these young men it seemed a great adventure. They did not pause to count the cost, but offered their services and their lives when their country called.

Almost as soon as war started, Australian troops and ships were sent to capture German New Guinea and other islands. Very quickly they succeeded in their task with the loss of only five men. Within three months the first part of the A.I.F. was ready to sail overseas. As you can imagine, the men were keen to be on the move. Ships from ports all over Australia were altered to transport these thousands of men. New Zealand forces joined ours at Albany in Western Australia, and together the ANZACs (members of the Australian and New Zealand Army Corps) steamed away from the little harbour on 1st November, 1914.

Eight days later the Royal Australian Navy fought its first battle.

The German cruiser *Emden* had caused a great deal of damage to Allied shipping, and she was sighted approaching little Cocos Island. The radio operator there sent a message through to the Australian convoy, and H.M.A.S. *Sydney*, one of our battle-cruisers, was ordered to "go after the enemy ship".

In a short space of time the excited troops heard *Sydney*'s message, "Am briskly engaging enemy." Loud cheering from the men on board followed this announcement. Then, about an hour later, the Commander's final message came through," *Emden* beached and done for." This was a proud moment indeed for the Australians.

Egypt had been chosen as the place where the ANZACs were to do their training and, after the long sea voyage, you may be sure they were happy to leave the ships at last. Here, in the land of the sphinx and the pyramids they marched, drilled, worked and sweltered for months. Flies, sand and heat were their constant enemies, but they carried on with determination. These men knew they had to be fit, for shortly their lives might depend upon their strength.

There were few regrets when orders to move finally came through. After some months in the desert, the ANZACs were not sorry to bid farewell to this barren land. They were keen, too, to get on with the job and at last they were to come face to face with the enemy. Their first important action was to be against the Turks on the Gallipoli Peninsula.

An attempt by the Allied navies to force a way through the Dardanelles had failed. Therefore, land forces including British, French and ANZAC troops were to be used. Their aim was to take Gallipoli and the Turkish capital, Constantinople.

How did these ANZACs feel on that still, moonlit night as they steamed out of the harbour to face the enemy for the first time? An eye-witness wrote:– They seemed "to be cheerful, quiet and confident. There was no sign of nerves or undue excitement." But, in the early morning of 25th April, there was to be excitement aplenty.

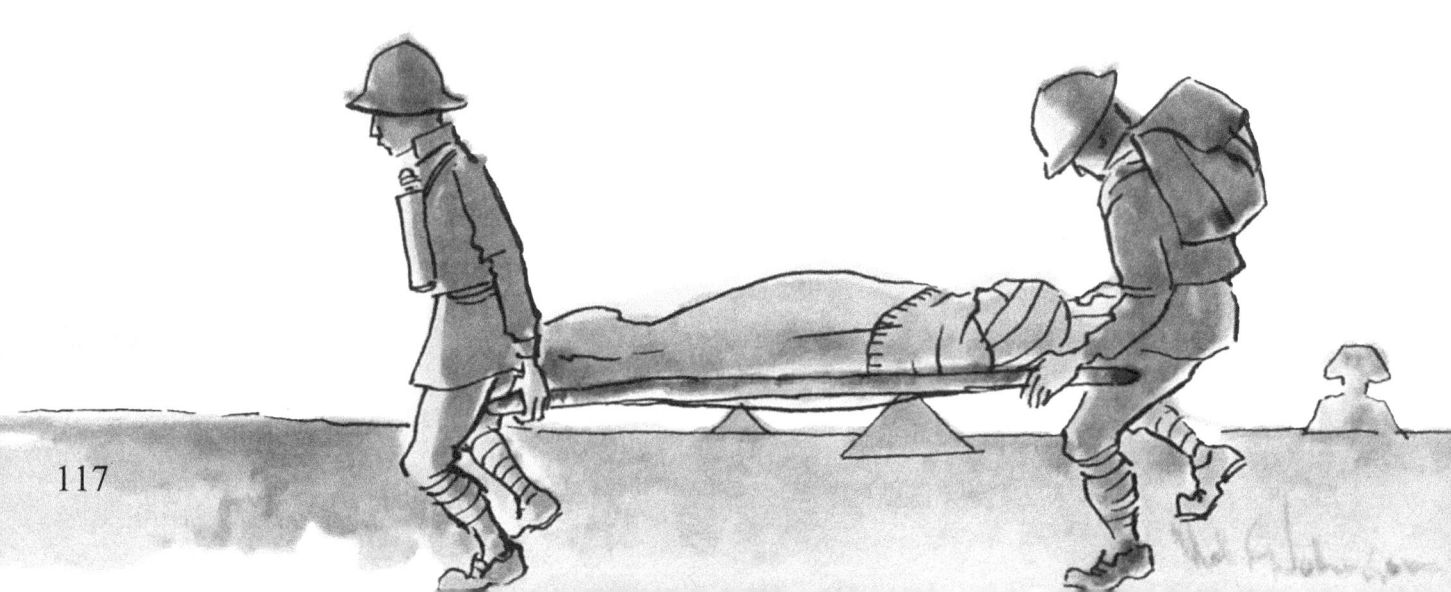

The ANZACs were landed by accident a kilometre farther north than was planned. The little boats to which they had been transferred splashed quietly through the calm waters. The silence was eerie. Suddenly, the enemy opened fire. Snipers' bullets rained down on men and boats. Leaping out into the shallow water, with rifles held high over their heads, the ANZACs fairly flew towards the enemy's gunfire. With fixed bayonets they fiercely attacked the Turks. However, units were broken up and everything became confused. The leaders were separated from their men, and it became impossible for a company to stay together.

The landing continued all day under heavy fire, for the Turks, expecting a land attack, had greatly increased their defences.

Arrival of the first big gun caused great excitement and much cheering from the men on the beach. Even the wounded, lying there waiting to be taken back to the transports, joined in the cheering.

Do you know that water had to be brought all the way from Egypt? Donkeys were used to carry it to the front line in kerosene tins. It was always scarce and very strictly rationed to each man. During the entire campaign the shortage of water was a great problem.

For many months the war on the peninsula continued. Ridges were taken, lost and retaken, but no worth-while advance was made. The wounded numbered thousands, and stretcher-bearers worked night and day. One of these brave men, John Simpson Kirkpatrick, became famous as "The Man with the Donkey". With his sturdy little mule, Duffy, he moved a great number of wounded men back to base hospitals and field ambulance stations. Simpson and Duffy had to face the constant danger of rifle fire and shrapnel, but their courage never failed. A sniper's bullet finally caused Simpson's death. Little Duffy returned to the base alone and was safely evacuated at the end of the campaign.

Many famous battles were fought at Gallipoli during the next six months, but the Turks held on fiercely.

Finally, the British leaders decided they would evacuate the Allied troops and thus end the struggle for the Dardanelles.

Plans were made to keep the evacuation a secret from the enemy, and all sorts of tricks were used to keep the Turks guessing. At dawn on 20th December the last little boats, laden with soldiers and supplies, left ANZAC Cove. Our men were safely off, farewelled by a huge blaze of light as the supply dumps exploded.

Of the Gallipoli campaign a journalist wrote, "In few other expeditions has the gallantry of the troops been more outstanding, or their hardships greater." After it had finished, the ANZACs fought gruelling campaigns for two years against the Germans in France. Here too they won a glorious reputation for their valour and fighting skill. One thing is certain: when the war ended on the 11th November, 1918, the ANZACs had won the admiration of the whole world, by their courage, their strength and their determination.

Australia, the nation, had played well her gallant part in the First World War, and when the peace treaties were drawn up Australia signed them as a separate nation. Later she took her place, along with the other members, in a newly formed League of Nations. This was established in the hope that the nations would in future be able to settle their differences by talking about them and not by fighting. Woodrow Wilson, President of the United States, was particularly anxious to have such an organization set up, and of him it has truly been said, "He lifted up the hearts of men and opened the gates of peace; and he did more, for he gave us the power to shut for ever the gates of war."

The League of Nations was a wonderful idea. If all men had followed Wilson's plan, the dreadful war that broke out in 1939 might never have occurred.

Chapter Thirteen
After World War 1

IN the years immediately following World War I, Australia continued to develop as both an agricultural and an industrial nation. Many of the men who had fought so well for their country were given farms, so that they could earn a living in the years of peace.

Each State had its own plan for Soldier Settlement. Sometimes the men were given farms in the drier western areas, where wheat could be sown; others had fruit, vegetable, or poultry farms. In order to provide these farms, State governments sometimes bought large estates and cut them up into smaller areas. Other farms were provided in new areas where no cultivation had been carried out before. Some soldiers were granted land in new irrigation areas such as Red Cliffs in Victoria or Griffith in the Murrumbidgee Irrigation Area. The building of great dams to store water made it possible to open up areas for irrigation which would otherwise have been useless, though unfortunately some soldier settlers were given land in country that was too dry and after a few years they had to abandon their holdings.

Men like the Chaffey brothers and Sir Samuel McCaughey had already shown the great advantages of proper irrigation. The Chaffey brothers had, in 1887, begun irrigation of land in the Mildura district of Victoria and in the Renmark area of South Australia, using water from the Murray River. McCaughey, by the year 1900, had built 320 kilometres of channels, so that his estate called North Yanco could be irrigated by water from the Murrumbidgee River.

Following the lead of such pioneers, governments of the different States began to plan irrigation areas and to build dams to make sure these areas had a reliable supply of water. The Burrinjuck dam is a good example. Built on the Murrumbidgee River in New South Wales the Burrinjuck was completed in 1927. When the giant wall was later enlarged and strengthened, experts estimated that the volume of water it was capable of conserving was equal to twice the volume in Sydney Harbour. This dam gives a reliable supply to the Murrumbidgee Irrigation Area, serves some of the country centres of population, and a power station at the dam produces hydro-electricity.

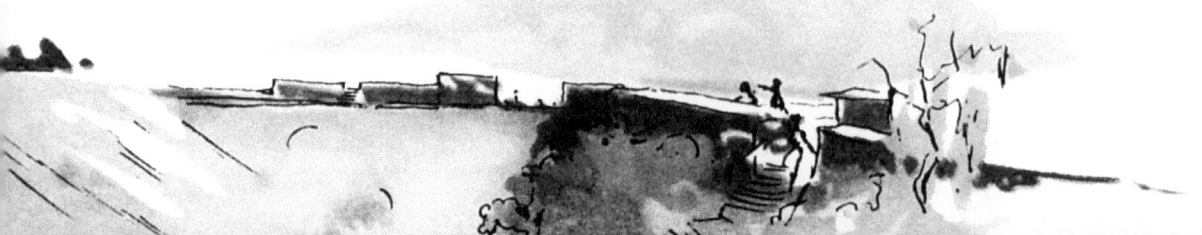

In Tasmania, with its heavy rainfall and steep mountain slopes, it is fairly easy to generate electricity from the power of falling water, so a huge hydro-electricity scheme was developed there. The mighty Waddamana power-station on the Ouse River was completed in 1923, and the great Tarraleah station on the Nive River began to generate electricity in 1938.

One industry to expand greatly during World War I, and in the years after the war, was the iron and steel industry. The Newcastle works of the Broken Hill Proprietary Co. (BHP) began production in 1915, and the iron and steel from its furnaces played an important part in Australia's war effort. After the war there was an increasing demand for steel and steel goods. Another company, Australian Iron and Steel Ltd, built a great new works at Port Kembla. They were opened in 1928 and continued to expand, especially after joining with BHP in 1935. In 1963 the huge number-four blast-furnace at Port Kembla broke the world's record for the amount of iron produced by the one furnace in a single day.

There were many Australian industries depending upon steel from Newcastle or Port Kembla. One of the most important was the automotive industry.

The very first Australian-built car was the Tarrant, built in 1905. Unfortunately this vehicle was unable to compete with those manufactured in other countries, and the automotive industry was not really important in Australia until 1925, when the Ford works at Geelong were opened. Some sections of the cars produced at Geelong were manufactured in Australia, but many of the parts were imported from the United States of America.

Australia's most popular car was the Holden. The Holden Company began by making motor bodies in South Australia, Victoria, and New South Wales. In 1931 the General Motors Corporation of the United States of America combined with the Holden Body Builders, and the company known as General Motors Holden Limited came into being. The first Holden car rolled off the assembly-line in 1948, and the car was an immediate success. Ten years later, 400,000 Holdens had been sold - many in Australia, but a great number were exported to other countries.

Today cars imported from other countries have made it difficult for manufacturing to continue in Australia but huge quantities of iron ore and coal are exported to other steel-making countries.

In 1999 BHP decided to close the steelworks in Newcastle but, under its new name (since 2003) of *Bluescope Steel* it has expanded into Asia, with development of new steel plants in China, Indonesia, Thailand and Vietnam. The Port Kembla Steelworks has continued to develop and it has now become one of the world's most successful and efficient steel plants.

Another exciting development after the 1914-18 war was the speedy improvement of the aeroplane as a means of travel and transport. Although Australia has never been an important manufacturer of aircraft, the part played by Australian airmen in the story of flight has been remarkable. Some of the greatest pioneers of the air have been Australians, and we should be proud of the achievements of these great men and women.

Even before the First World War, Lawrence Hargrave had carried out many experiments to discover important principles of flight. On the south coast of New South Wales his kites, which looked like a number of boxes joined together and were therefore called box-kites, had discovered secrets that were to be of special help to Wilbur and Orville Wright of the United States for their flights in the world's first "heavier-than-air" machine.

Once the war was over, men could see the advantages to be gained by speedy aircraft transport from one country to another. The Australian Government offered a prize of £10,000 (about $25,000) to the first all-Australian crew to fly from Great Britain to Australia. After a most dramatic flight, four men claimed the prize. They were Ross and Keith Smith, who were brothers, and their two friends, Bennett and Shiers. The flight was made in 1919 in a Vickers-Vimy biplane, and it took twenty-eight days. The airmen had to nurse their aircraft through rough weather, attacks by hawks, and damage caused by landing on rough or muddy airstrips. At Pisa, in Italy, there was a line of trees at the end of the airstrip and it seemed the Vickers would not be able to climb quickly enough to clear them. Bennett decided to climb to the tail of the aircraft and swing there, thus pointing the nose farther into the air. This action was successful, and Bennett was pulled aboard the Vickers after the plane had swept over the tops of the trees.

Following their successful flight, the two Smith brothers were knighted and Bennett and Shiers were awarded the Air Force Medal.

Nine years later another Australian pilot, Bert Hinkler, made the first solo England to Australia flight. Called the "Lone Eagle", Hinkler used a tiny Avro-Avian aircraft and completed the journey in sixteen days. The English journal, Punch, celebrated this success by publishing a full-page cartoon, under which was written:

> "*Hinkle, Hinkle, little star,*
> *Sixteen days and here you are!*

With Mr. Punch's congratulations on your great solo performance."

Of all Australian aviators, perhaps the most famous was Sir Charles Kingsford Smith. It was in 1917 that "Smithy" first flew as a fighter pilot. For gallantry in action he won the Military Cross. When wounded in the foot and unable to continue active duty as a fighter pilot, Smithy became an instructor so that he could teach others. In 1928 he set out with three friends, to prove that an aeroplane could travel across the immense distances of the Pacific Ocean.

Smithy's friends on the Pacific flight were Charles Ulm, Harry Lyon, and Jim Warner. The four men had bought a single-winged, three-engined aeroplane and had called it the *Southern Cross*. In it they planned to fly from San Francisco in the United States to Brisbane in Australia. There were to be only two stops in between, one at Honolulu and the other at Fiji.

The four pioneers had no trouble in reaching Honolulu, but the next part of their journey gave them some worrying moments. They had to fly through several storms. During one of these storms the lights on the dashboard suddenly blacked out, and the plane's instruments could not be seen. Fortunately, the airmen were carrying a torch and light from this torch helped the fliers to reach their next stop, Suva, capital of Fiji.

When they landed on a small oval in Suva thousands of Fijians swarmed across to welcome them. There had been a lunar eclipse the night before and some of the Fijians told stories of seeing the *Wangu-Vuka* ("bird-ship") hovering in the sky and deciding to rest on the moon before landing the next day. It was quite an amazing story, with some of the Fijian people being quite convinced the airmen had used grappling hooks to catch the moon.

To reach Brisbane from Fiji the pioneers had to fly only 2,900 kilometres. As the *Southern Cross* had already covered some 8,000 kilometres, it seemed that this last "hop" would not be very hard. However, a raging storm was to make this final part of the journey very difficult and dangerous indeed.

Lashing at the aircraft, the fury of the storm caused the *Southern Cross* to pitch and lurch in the darkness. The windscreen was leaking badly and the two pilots, Smithy and Ulm, were soaked to the skin. Soon they were numb with cold.

"Anything that is worth having is worth a fight," Smithy was later to write in one of his books. He and the other three pioneers fought the storm with the only weapons they had — skill and courage. When, after a grim struggle, the men saw the rain clouds pass away they should have been able to relax, but there was a new danger — they were running short of fuel. How relieved they must have been to sight the coast of Australia. At last the *Southern Cross* was brought to rest at Brisbane, and the Pacific Ocean had been crossed.

During his lifetime Smithy flew many trips that thrilled the world. He was knighted in 1932 for his many great deeds, but if Sir Charles Kingsford Smith had flown only one of those many flights — the flight from San Francisco to Brisbane — he would still deserve to be remembered as one of the really great pioneers in the story of flight.

Pioneering work in Australia's air story was also done by many other men. Two of these are worthy of special mention. They are Sir Hudson Fysh and Dr John Flynn. Fysh, with the great help of his friend, P. J. McGinniss used two ex-World-War-I machines to begin the service known as the Queensland and Northern Territory Aerial Services Limited. Their plan was to serve with fast aerial transport the widely separated places of Australia's vast inland.

Today, the company which they began is known the world over by its initials, QANTAS. It has served Australia well in times of peace and war.

It was largely through the vision and determination of one man, the Reverend Dr John Flynn, that a Flying Doctor Service was begun in 1928. Today modern aircraft and improved methods of communication make it possible for all people in Australia's inland to be within reach of medical attention and up-to-date airports are able to cope with huge new aircraft linking our nation with the rest of the world.

As we have seen, the period between the two world wars was, generally, one of progress and development for Australia. There was one short time, in the early 1930s, when Australia, along with most other countries in the world suffered a serious economic depression. This was a time when many men walked the streets looking for work and their families were hungry because there were just no jobs to be had. Without money, without jobs and without hope, men found these to be desperate years indeed. There were plenty of goods to be bought, but people just did not have the money to buy them. Many thousands had to receive the "dole," that is, an amount of money provided by the Government. The dole was hardly enough to keep body and soul together, and people were relieved when conditions gradually improved and men were again able to work in steady employment.

Chapter Fourteen

The Second World War

ALTHOUGH the League of Nations accomplished a great deal after the First World War, there was one thing it could not do: it could not stop greed from having power over the hearts and minds of some men. There were still those in the world who wanted to grasp as much power as possible for themselves and their countries. One such man was Adolf Hitler.

The German people had been treated harshly by other nations after World War I and they had suffered greatly during the depression. Many of them were very ready to listen to and believe Hitler when he told them that they were the "master race", and would again be great and powerful. He made plans to overrun the rest of Europe and eventually to make the German people the masters of Europe and perhaps of the world. Some countries decided to side with Hitler, while others, including Great Britain, were determined to stop him.

When Britain found it necessary to declare war on Nazi Germany, the Australian Government immediately made the decision to once again help the Mother Country. Mr Menzies (later Sir Robert Menzies) was Prime Minister at the time, and he made a broadcast declaring that Australia was at war.

Later, when Britain was being savagely attacked in the Battle of Britain, Mr Menzies telegraphed this message to Mr Churchill, "The Mother Country may be assured that in every part of the Empire, and in no part more than in Australia, there is a resolution to do all, bear all and spend all for the success of our most holy cause."

Food supplies, weapons and armed forces were sent to help Britain and, at the same time, to keep the enemy from approaching our shores. Men and women from all walks of life came to swell the ranks. Thousands of them were to give their lives before the war came finally to an end. Australia deeply mourned the tragic loss of life that occurred on 19th November, 1941, when the cruiser *HMAS Sydney* was lost in a battle with the German raider, *Kormoran*. Both ships were sunk but, distressingly, all 645 men on board the *Sydney* were lost. Where the wrecks and brave sailors lay remained a mystery until 2008 when both wrecks were found at last, close to Geraldton , off the coast of Western Australia.

It seemed, at first, that the best way Australia could help the war effort was to send supplies to her allies and to send armed forces to Europe. Australians fought in many areas during the war, gallantly and with determination carrying out their duties. The Australian Army was used especially in Greece and Crete, and at Tobruk where, for eight months, the men withstood a determined attack by the German Afrika Korps which was led by the brilliant Field-Marshal Rommel. Stubbornly holding on to their positions in the trenches the Australians were called by the enemy "The Rats of Tobruk". It was not meant to be a compliment but the men of the AIF treated it as one and later were proud to be known throughout the world as "The Rats of Tobruk".

The gallant Australians then took part in the successful defence of the Suez Canal, which was to bring to an end the plans of the enemy for a southward advance.

When Singapore fell as a result of Japanese attack in February, 1942, Australia's war plans had to be altered. Mr Curtin, who was the Prime Minister then, decided to bring our soldiers and other forces back from Europe, so that Australia herself could be defended. "We are determined," said Mr. Curtin "that Australia shall not go." But the Japanese had further successes and came yet closer to Australia.

Finally, Japanese bombers began to raid Australian territory. Darwin, Wyndham, Broome, Derby, and Katherine were all bombed and, for the first time in her history, Australia was in great danger of invasion.

In May, 1942, a huge Japanese fleet was on its way toward our shores. The enemy ships included transports, aircraft carriers, cruisers and smaller craft. Important cities on Australia's eastern coast were in very great danger indeed. Australian people are forever grateful that, in this dark hour of need, we were not left to fight alone.

The American fleet in the Pacific, aided by the Australian ships, HMAS *Australia* and HMAS *Hobart*, gave battle to the Japanese fleet in the Coral Sea, on 4th May. After a fierce engagement, waged mainly by aircraft from the two fleets, the Japanese were turned back. In this battle both fleets suffered heavy losses, but in spite of the losses to the Japanese fleet the danger to Australia still existed, for, having thrust toward the mainland by capturing islands to the north-west of Australia, the Japanese had landed in New Guinea and had fought their way across the Owen Stanley Range until they were in a position to menace Australia herself.

A counter-attack against the enemy in New Guinea was begun in September, 1942. It was on 6th September that two Australian brigades fought a famous battle with the Japanese at Milne Bay on the south-eastern tip of Papua. They were trying to capture the airfield. Had they succeeded they would have been able to use it to launch land-based bombing attacks against Australia. The Australians fought desperately and, for the first time, defeated the Japanese and forced the enemy to withdraw by sea. Gradually the Japanese were driven back over the

Owen Stanley Range. The steep trail followed by our men is known as the Kokoda Track, and the mud, slush, disease and sickness which dogged their steps made the battle against the Japanese even more difficult. With determination, and often displaying extreme courage in the presence of danger, the Australians drove the enemy back, saving the sunburnt country in the south from invasion.

Once defeated in New Guinea, the Japanese Army was pushed farther and farther back toward Japan itself. In August, 1945, World War II came to an end with the surrender of Japan. Germany had already surrendered in May.

There were many examples of outstanding courage displayed by the men of Australia's armed forces during World War II. A score of these men were awarded the *Victoria Cross*, which is the highest decoration for gallantry possible for a member of the Commonwealth. Space permits us to mention just a few of these brave men.

Corporal Jack Edmondson, though mortally wounded, used his bayonet to deal with five attacking enemy soldiers at Tobruk. He and six others drove back twenty Germans, who had broken through the Australian lines.

In the New Guinea campaign several Australians won the Victoria Cross, one being Sergeant Thomas Derrick, who, single-handed, wiped out ten enemy machine-gun posts. It was on the Kokoda Track that Private Bruce Kingsbury also won his Victoria Cross. He charged a nest of Japanese machine-gun posts, firing his Bren gun from the hip and clearing a path through the enemy lines before being shot down by a sniper's bullet.

It was at Milne Bay, in New Guinea, that three enemy machine-gun posts were silenced by the courageous, single-handed assault of Corporal John French. It was in Borneo that Private Leslie Starcevich was successful in wiping out four enemy machine-gun posts. Firing his Bren gun from the hip, he made his attack without regard for his own safety.

The soldiers I have mentioned, and many others, won their Victoria Crosses for amazing gallantry in the face of the enemy. Sailors and airmen from our land were also highly decorated for their bravery.

Lieutenant-Commander Rankin and the men of the little sloop, *Yarra*, engaged seven Japanese ships in a courageous, but hopelessly unequal battle. Rankin did not try to escape, but instead steered his course steadily and truly straight toward the enemy, hoping to keep them busy so that three unarmed merchant ships, being escorted by the *Yarra*, might make their escape. Most of the men on board the *Yarra*, including the courageous Rankin, lost their lives in the battle. Thirteen only were to live to tell the tale. Rankin was awarded the Victoria Cross for his devotion to duty and his selfless action in trying to defend the unarmed merchant ships.

Flight-Sergeant Middleton won his Victoria Cross in 1942. After bombing Turin, in northern Italy, he turned for England where he was based. His aircraft had been badly damaged during the raid, and Middleton was shockingly injured. Yet he was determined to get his men to safety. For 2,500 pain-filled kilometres he piloted his aircraft back toward the coast of England. There he ordered his crew to bale out. Middleton knew that there was barely enough fuel left for him to land, and that he was too weak, anyway, to bring the bomber in safely to land. So that he would not crash in any place where other people might be hurt, Middleton turned his plane for the ocean, and minutes later crashed into the sea.

Chapter Fifteen
Advance Australia

WHEN at last the war was over, people throughout the world wished only for peace. The United Nations Organization, already working when peace came, is continually trying to keep the peace throughout the world. Australia is a member of the United Nations, and the Australian people have worked hard to help other nations less fortunate than our own. Money, food supplies, materials and trained advisers have been made available when needed.

In order to help keep the peace in our own part of the world, Australia signed agreements with other nations. Two important agreements were the South-East Asia Treaty Organization (known as SEATO), and the Australia, New Zealand, United States Pact (known as ANZUS). The nations signing SEATO were the United States, Great Britain, France, the Philippines, Thailand, Australia, and New Zealand. These nations pledged support for one another if ever any of them were to be attacked. At the same time the treaty expressed a "desire to live in peace with all peoples and all governments". This treaty was abolished in 1977.

Unfortunately Australia has been involved in a number of conflicts since World War II. Among the worst of these have been the conflict in Korea (1950-1953), the War in Vietnam (1965-1972); the conflict in Afghanistan and the war which began in Iraq in 2003. Although many Australians have had serious doubts about our participation in these conflicts our government in each case has felt it was important to support our ally, the United States of America. However, in time the people of the USA came to believe the attacks upon the Vietnamese people and upon the people of Iraq were unwise and regrettable.

The Australian servicemen and women who have taken part in these conflicts have performed their duties honourably and courageously. One outstanding example of their courage was the battle that took place at Nui Dat on 18th August, 1966. A small group of Australians was ambushed in a rubber tree plantation by about 2,500 North Vietnamese fighters. Within minutes and in pouring rain a third of the Australian soldiers were dead or wounded. The remainder fired rapidly at the enemy and called for shells to be fired into the Viet Cong positions, even though they were so close there was a risk the Australians would also be hit.

The Australians were soon running out of ammunition and so, in a daring manoeuvre RAAF helicopters swooped in and dropped ammunition wrapped in blankets. This made it possible for the Australians to continue fighting until other units of Australians arrived in armoured personnel carriers (APCs) and took the battle right up to the Viet Cong, who then started to retreat in the gathering darkness. A small group of 100 Australians had kept at bay and finally forced the retreat of 2,500 Viet Cong.

Fortunately no enemy has been able to land troops onto Australian soil. However Australians have had to deal with the old enemies of fire and flood and drought and a number of other challenges.

During the bush-fire season, which begins in Spring and lasts until late Autumn, we often hear of a bushfire occurring somewhere in our country. These bushfires move quickly through the bush, leaping high in the air and spreading through the crowns of the trees, leaving widespread destruction. The oil in the leaves of gum trees (eucalyptus trees) makes them burn fast and hot. Strong summer winds fan the flames, with disastrous consequences.

Flooding rains are also a hazard that Australians have come to accept. One notable flood occurred in June 2007 when the Hunter region had a tremendous storm. After less than twenty-four hours of rain Newcastle's main streets looked like fast-flowing rivers. Surf life savers on their surf skis combed the streets saving people who had been trapped in their cars or houses because of flash flooding. An enormous ship, the Pasha Bulker, a bulk coal carrier, ran aground at Newcastle's Nobbys Beach, due to high seas and strong winds. After many attempts and some extra help from Melbourne tugboats the ship was finally pulled free three weeks later. The whole region was on flood alert and Newcastle was declared a natural disaster zone.

Droughts, which sometimes last for a number of years, have also been a great challenge to the Australian people, especially the farmers who see their crops fail and have to sell their sheep and cattle or see them starve.

Our dry and thirsty land requires much water for household use and agriculture and for many other industries. This has led to problems in rivers such as the Murray-Darling due to massive clearing of vegetation and an ever-increasing demand for water. This has caused the salt table to rise, resulting in a very worrying salinity problem. Leading scientific groups, such as the CSIRO, are working hard to find solutions to these problems. Green-house gas emissions and global warming are immense problems for Australia and the world. The Federal and State Governments and scientific groups are working hard to try to bring these problems under control.

Sometimes cyclones and hurricanes strike the Australian coastline with tremendous force. It was early on Christmas morning in 1974 that Cyclone Tracy hit Darwin and ripped the city apart, destroying many of the buildings, killing more than 65 people and injuring another thousand. Within one week 10,000 people had to be evacuated and billeted out around Australia. About 11,000 of the adults of Darwin stayed to help a magnificent team of volunteers clean up and begin to reconstruct the city.

It was on 14th October, 1968 that an earthquake measuring seven on the Richter Scale flattened the township of Meckering in Western Australia. Some buildings in Perth were damaged and the quake was felt as far away as Kalgoorlie, 800 kilometres to the east. In the 1989

Newcastle earthquake thirteen people died. More than 160 people sustained injuries and over 10,000 buildings in Newcastle suffered from slight to substantial damage. Over a billion dollars was paid out by insurance companies. The earthquake, measuring 5.6 on the Richter Scale once again shattered the myth that disastrous earthquakes do not occur in Australia.

Some of Australia's problems have been caused when the land has not been used appropriately or when animals or plants have been introduced from abroad. Cane toads, foxes, rabbits and even camels, have all been introduced either to provide "sport" or to try to solve some agricultural problem. In every case they now compete for food with our native animals. Wild horses in the Snowy Mountains, known as brumbies, destroy large areas of land. Cats and dogs have been introduced to provide comfort and companionship for us but when deserted by their owners cats and dogs sometimes become wild again. Feral cats cause great harm to native animals and birds and packs of wild dogs attack the livestock of farmers.

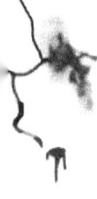

Over the years removal of native trees has been necessary so that farming and agriculture could flourish. However, such clearing of the land has also brought real problems. Erosion of the soil by water and wind and the removal of the habitats of native animals and birds are two examples of such problems. People in all countries are beginning to realise that the wholesale removal of native forests is contributing to worldwide climatic problems. However, even though remaining native forests in Australia are now only a fraction of the forests that existed before European settlement began, further clearing will continue to take place unless prevented by political leaders.

Fortunately most Australian people are becoming more aware of the need to conserve our beautiful sunburnt country. Steps are being taken to preserve some of its natural habitats by having World Heritage Listing for areas around Australia. We currently have seventy-seven listed. Some well-known ones are The Great Barrier Reef, Tasmanian Wilderness and Kakadu National park.

In many ways Australia has grown quite amazingly since World War II. Population is one example of this growth. In 1945 there were only seven million people living in Australia, and now the number is more than twenty million. This great increase has resulted largely from the immigration policy adopted by the Government. Since the war people from many different countries have come to live in our land. Many have come from the United Kingdom and other European countries but others have come to us from New Zealand and islands of the Pacific; from Africa, Asia and countries of the Middle East. Since 1945 several million migrants have been welcomed to our shores. As New Australians, they have helped this country to develop.

Sadly, ever since the arrival of The First Fleet in 1788 Aboriginal Australians have often been treated very badly. Many "White" Australians have regretted such treatment. On 3 June, 1992, the High Court of Australia delivered its landmark Mabo decision which rewrote the Australian common law and gave a massive boost to the struggle for Aboriginal Land Rights. Put simply, the decision said that under Australian law and under certain conditions Indigenous people could have rights to land — rights that existed before colonisation and which still existed. This right is called *native title*.

Even after the High Court decision the Mabo Bill had to be passed by Parliament and the Prime Minister, Paul Keating, found that the Opposition parties would make passage of the bill very difficult. When it went to the Senate this opposition was intense and Senator Evans had

to be on his feet for more than fifty hours before the bill was finally passed around midnight on 21st December, 1993. When it *was* passed crowds packing the public and press galleries stood and applauded.

On May 28th, in the year 2000, hundreds of thousands took part in the *People's Walk for Reconciliation* in all capital cities and were glad when, on the very first day of sitting of the newly-elected parliament in 2008, at that time Prime Minister of Australia, Mr Kevin Rudd, delivered a heart-felt apology to the Aboriginal people, especially to those who were known as members of "the Stolen Generations". This apology was supported by the Opposition parties and by the great majority of Australians.

On that day thousands from across the nation gathered outside Parliament House and at vantage points in other centres to witness this historic event on large television screens. It was very fitting that, the day before Mr Rudd said "Sorry" to the Aboriginal race, members of the local Aboriginal people had performed a *Welcome to the Nation* ceremony at Parliament House.

Many new manufacturing industries have developed in Australia, but agriculture, grazing and mining are still very important to the country's economy. Our exports include minerals, wool, beef and lamb, live sheep and cattle and wheat.

Australia is the world's leading exporter of lead, diamonds and bauxite (from which aluminium is made), and is an important exporter of iron ore, gold and silver, zinc and tin.

Almost all the world's best opals are mined in this country and Australia has the world's largest deposits of uranium.

There have been discoveries of oil and gas that have helped supply our needs. Over the years wells producing oil were sunk at Rough Range, near Exmouth Gulf in Western Australia and at the Moonie field in Queensland. A 310 kilometre-long pipeline was built to move the oil from Moonie to the port of Brisbane.

South Australia and Victoria also produce some petroleum and in South Australia, and especially along the northwest coast of Western Australia are vast fields of natural gas.

It was in 1932 that the Sydney Harbour Bridge was opened and it is famous throughout the world, partly because it was a wonderful engineering achievement but also because it is the centre-piece of the wonderfully colourful fireworks that have welcomed the beginning of each New Year. These joyful occasions are telecast around the world.

In October, 2013 sixteen tall sailing ships and modern warships from thirteen other countries joined in celebrations with Australian warships to commemorate the centenary of the Royal Australian Navy. The highlight of the celebration was the evening of the 5th of October when the night was lit up with a spectacular fireworks display from the Harbour Bridge, Fort Denison, Cockatoo Island, city rooftops and decks of R.A.N warships. A magnificent lightshow spectacular was flashed onto the white sails of the Opera House to tell everyone the proud history of our navy.

The most daring engineering development ever undertaken in Australia was probably the Snowy Mountains Scheme which alters the flow of the Snowy River and its tributary, the Eucumbene, from a generally south-easterly direction towards the drier areas of the west. To achieve this, seven enormous dams were built, more than 110 kilometres of underground tunnels, sometimes nearly 1500 metres beneath the surface, were constructed and seventeen power stations were built to produce hydro-electricity. Thousands of workers from many different nations were employed by the Snowy Mountains Authority to accomplish this incredible engineering feat.

When full the mighty Eucumbene Dam holds back more than eight times the water in Sydney Harbour. As it is gradually released the water flows westward through tunnels to the Tumut and Murrumbidgee Rivers. It falls 1000 metres and passes through five hydro-electric power stations on the way.

Other great achievements include the building of a great dam on the Ord River in the north of Western Australia; the construction of splendid motorways and railways linking all parts of the land; the continued development of airports and the erection of fine buildings including magnificent sky-scrapers in all our major cities and especially the beautiful Sydney Opera House, famous throughout the world, opened in 1973 by Her Majesty, Queen Elizabeth II.

In 1993 Sydney won the rights to host the XXVII Olympiad or Olympic games, in 2000. A whole Olympic village called Newington was constructed to house the athletes and officials. The most up-to-date sports facilities were built. "Green" energy was used wherever possible and Newington was, in the year 2000, the largest solar suburb in Australia.

It was a very proud moment for Australians when Cathy Freeman, an Aboriginal gold medalist, lit the Olympic flame. Australian athletes gave extraordinary performances at these games winning fifty eight medals, and were placed fourth on the medal tally. Since then our athletes have continued to bring great credit to our nation.

In so many ways Australian people are remembering the words of the song written in 1878 by Peter Dodds McCormick. It is called "Advance Australia Fair", and it is fitting that it should have been chosen as the national song of this developing, sunburnt country. These are the rousing words of that song's first stanza:

> Australians all let us rejoice,
> For we are young and free,
> We've golden soil and wealth for toil,
> Our home is girt by sea.
> Our land abounds in nature's gifts of
>   beauty rich and rare,
> In history's page let every stage
> Advance Australia Fair.
> In joyful strains then let us sing
> Advance Australia Fair.

INDEX

Aboriginal guides: Colbee; Charlie Tara; Boladeree;
  Wylie; Carley & Harry; Jackey-Jackey   89
Aboriginal Legend: *Bohra, The Kangaroo*   10-11
Aborigines   10-20; 89; 114; 135-136
Afghanistan   131
American War of Independence   38
Anthony Van Diemenslandt   26
ANZACs   116-119
ANZUS   131
Australian Alps   80
Australian Imperial Force   115
Australian Iron and Steel Company   110

Ballarat   98;102
Banks, Sir Joseph 34; 37; 38
Barton, Edmund   112
Bass, George   53-61
Bathurst   69
Bathurst Plains   68
Batman, John   91
Battle of Britain   127
Bayley, Arthur Wellesley (and W. Ford) 92; 102
Bendigo   98; 102
Bligh, William   50-52
Bluescope Steel   122
Bonner, Neville (Senator)   20
Botany Bay   34
Bourke, Sir Richard   91
Bradshaw (Gwion) Figures   142
Brisbane, Sir Thomas   75; 77
Broken Hill Proprietary Company (B.H.P.)   121
Buddha   10
Burke, Robert O'Hara and Wills, William   88
Burrinjuck Dam   120
Bushrangers: Thunderbolt; Moonlight; Ned Kelly 103

Cape of Good Hope   21
Chaffey Brothers   120
Christ (*Jesus*)   10
Churchill, Sir Winston   127
Cobb & CO.   103-104
Collins, Colonel David   90
Cook, Lieutenant James (*Endeavour*) 31-38
Coolgardie   92; 102
Coral Sea (Battle of the Coral Sea)   128
Cox, William   68-69
Cunningham, Alan 75; 76; 77
Curtin, John   127
Cyclone Tracy   133

Dampier, Willem (*Cygnet; Roebuck*) 28-29
Darwin (bombed by Japanese. Also bombed were
  Wyndham, Broome, Derby & Katherine) 128
Deakin, Alfred   113
Depression (*The Great Depression*) 125
Derrick, Sergeant Thomas V.C.   129
Diaz, Bartolomeo 21
"Dictation Test"   114
Diprotodon 12

Edmondson, Corporal Jack V.C   129
Emden (German ship sunk by *HMAS Sydney*) 116
Engineering achievements 137-138
Eureka Stockade 101
Evans, George   67-68; and with Oxley 71-77
Eyre, Edward John   88

Farrer, William   108
Fawkner, John Pascoe   91
Fisher, Andrew   115
Flinders, Matthew (*Tom Thumb; Tom Thumb 11;
  Investigator*)   53-63
Flood and fire and famine (drought) 132-133
Flynn, Rev. Dr. John (Flying Doctor Service) 125
Ford Works at Geelong 121
Forrest, John   88
French, Corporal John V.C. 130
Fysh, Sir Hudson and P.J.McGinniss 125

Gallipoli 117-118
General Motors Holden   121
Genyornis   12
Giles, Ernest   88
Gold; Discovery of   94-102
Gregory, A.C. (Sir Augustus Charles) 88
Greenway, Francis   64; 70
Griffin, Walter Burley   113
Grose, Major Francis   47-49
Gulden Seepard   24

Hancock, Lang 92
Hargrave, Lawrence 122
Hargraves, Edward Hammond 95-96
Hartog, Dirk (*Eendracht*) 23
Henty Brothers   90-91
Hinkler, Bert   123
Hitler, Adolf   110

HMAS Sydney   116
HMAS Sydney 11 127
Hope, Louis   109
Hopetoun (Lord) First Governor-General 112
Hoskins, George and Charles 110
Hotham, Captain Charles 99; 100
Howard, John   90
Hovell, William   77-83
Hume, Hamilton   77-83
Hunter, John   50-53

Iraq; war in Iraq   131

Jansz, Willem (*Duyfken*) 23
Johnston, Major (Lieutenant-Governor) 52

Kalgoorlie 92; 102

Keating, Paul   135
Kennedy, Edmund 88
King, Philip Gidley 50; 53
Kingsbury, Private Bruce V.C. 129
Kirkpatrick, John Simpson (and "Duffy") 118
Kokoda Track   129
Korea; war in   131

Lalor, Peter   100

La Perouse (*La Boussole* and *L'Astrolabe*) 41
Lawson, Lieutenant William 65
League of Nations 119
Leichhardt, Friedrich Wilhelm Ludwig 88
Lord, Simeon 64

Mabo (Native Title Bill) 135

Macarthur, John 47; 52; 64; 106
McCaughey, Sir Samuel   120
McCormick, Peter Dodds   139
McLeay, George   86
McKay, Hugh   108
Macquarie, Colonel Lachlan 52; 64-74
Marsden, Rev. Samuel 106
Meckering earthquake 133
Megafauna 12
Menzies, Sir Robert 127
Middleton, Flight Sergeant V.C. 130
Milne Bay 128; 130
Mort, Thomas Sutcliffe 106-108
Murrumbidgee Irrigation Area 120

Namatjira, Albert 20
Newcastle   134
New Holland   28; 29; 30
Nui Dat   131-132

Olympic Games   138
Owen Stanley Range   128; 129
Oxley, John   69; 71-77; 85

Parkes, Sir Henry 111-112
Pamphlett, Tom (and Parsons and Finnegan) 76-77
Procoptodon   12

Rankin, Lieutenant-Commander V.C. 130
Redfern, Dr William   64
Ridley, John   108
Rock paintings (Bradshaw Figures) 142
Rommel; German Field-Marshal
     (*Afrika Korps*)   127
Rough Range (and Moonie) 136
Rudd, Kevin   136
Rum; trade in 48-50; 52

Scott, Thomas   109
SEATO   131
Shortland, John   59
Smith, Sir Charles Kingsford in "*Southern Cross*" with Charles Ulm: Harry Lyon and Jim Warner 123
Smith, Robert   108
Smith, Ross and Keith (with Bennett and Shiers) 122-123
Spice Islands   22
Starcevich, Private Leslie V.C. 130
Stirling, Captain James   91
St Lawrence River   31
Strzelecki, Count Paul   88; 94
Stuart, John McDouall   88
Sturt, Captain Charles   84-87
Sutherland Point (Thorby Sutherland) 35

Tarraleah Power Station   121

Tarrant 121
Tasman, Abel Janszoon (*Heemskerk and Zeehaen*) 25
Tobruk (and "the Rats of Tobruk") 127
Tom Thumb   53
Tom Thumb 11   54
Transit of Venus   32

Uluru (formerly known as "Ayer's Rock") 89

Van Diemen, Anthony   25
Vasco da Gama   21
Vietnam   131
Vlamingh, Willem de   24

Waddamana Power Station   121
Warburton, Colonel Peter Egerton   88
Wentworth, William Charles   65-67
"White Australia" Policy   113-114
Wilson, Woodrow   119
World Heritage Listings   134
World War 1   115-118
World War 11   126-130

This photograph shows one of the many famous Bradshaw or "Gwion" rock paintings of the Kimberley. They are many thousands of years old and these twirling, dancing, tasselled figures tell us much about the society and culture of the ancient people of the Kimberley area.

Photograph kindly supplied by John Bradshaw.
(See "A Kimberley Adventure. Rediscovering the Bradshaw Figures" by Adrian Parker, John Bradshaw and Chris Done." Gecko Books 2007.)

www.ingramcontent.com/pod-product-compliance
Lightning Source LLC
Chambersburg PA
CBHW041714290426
44110CB00024B/2827